SPEAKING ILL OF THE DEAD

Jerks in Colorado History

Phyllis J. Perry

Guilford, Connecticut

To buy books in quantity for corporate use
or incentives, call **(800) 962-0973**
or e-mail **premiums@GlobePequot.com**.

Text design by Sheryl P. Kober
Project editor: Kristen Mellitt
Layout artist: Kevin Mak

Library of Congress Cataloging-in-Publication Data is available on file.

ISBN 978-0-7627-2705-6

Printed in the United States of America

10 9 8 7 6 5 4 3 2 1

Contents

Introduction

What is a "jerk" and how does one qualify to be one? According to Webster's, a jerk is "a despicable or worthless person." But there is more than one way to achieve "jerkdom" and to be included within the covers of this little volume.

As Abraham Lincoln wrote, "Character is like a tree and reputation like its shadow. The shadow is what we think of it; the tree is the real thing." It can be hard to reveal the true character of a historical figure. Sometimes single acts stain a lifetime of otherwise worthy accomplishments. In skimming through the names of the men and women included in this book, you may be surprised to find among these "jerks" some whom you consider heroes or heroines. Don't be shocked, for even a hero can sometimes behave like a jerk.

Does one false step make a jerk? If so, don't we all qualify? Fortunately, although most people err frequently, not much notice is taken of these mistakes or periods of misbehaving. But that's not the case with well-known historical figures, who, Lincoln also notes, "cannot escape history." Fair or not, we have different standards for public figures.

Colonel John Chivington may have been a hero at Glorieta Pass, but he was in command during a historical event at Sand Creek that most people call a massacre. He qualifies as a jerk. John Charles Frémont led three successful expeditions into the unknown and poorly mapped West, for which he was considered a national hero. He achieved jerk status when he failed badly in his leadership and lost more than a third of his men during a fourth disastrous expedition. His guide, Bill Williams, shares this dubious distinction.

The Earl of Dunraven served the United Kingdom well, but in his dishonest land grab of thousands of acres and driving off of honest settlers near Estes Park, he behaved like a jerk. The earl's good friend, Griffith Evans, was a delightful innkeeper most of the time, but when he drunkenly and without warning shot and killed Rocky Mountain Jim Nugent, Evans proved himself to be a jerk.

Bat Masterson and Doc Holliday were known as worthy law officers, but they were jerks when they acted as mere guns-for-hire during the Colorado Railroad War. Tom Horn may have been hung for a crime he didn't commit, but he was guilty of ambushing and murdering men for $500 a head. Notorious Denver madams Jennie Rogers and Mattie Silks looked out for their girls, but one framed and blackmailed a man to get the money she needed for a new bordello, and the other more than once fired her revolver willy-nilly to scare off rivals. The madams earned for themselves a rightful claim to jerkdom.

Perhaps political ambition temporarily clouded the judgment of Mayor Ben Stapleton and Governor Clarence Morley, leading them to accept and promote the worst tenets of the Colorado Ku Klux Klan headed by Grand Dragon John Galen Locke, one of history's greatest jerks. Their ambition and poor judgment led to a departure from basic decent principles and showed these men behaving like jerks in spite of other worthy accomplishments. H. A. W. Tabor, the Silver King, built an empire of mines and opera houses, but he also bought a senate seat for thirty days to stage an elaborate wedding for his new love after scorning his wife.

In Grand Lake the county commissioners were at each other's throats; nothing unusual there. But their bickering caused Sheriff Charles Royer and Undersheriff William Redman to kill off half their political opponents one Fourth of July.

Although he was always a soft touch for a worthy cause, Soapy Smith was still a jerk of a con man through and through. Alferd Packer, afflicted with epilepsy, may have started lying to hide his medical condition. He continued lying until it was impossible to learn the truth about his role when a small band of miners were trapped by snow in the mountains. Queen Ann Bassett was only one of many cattle rustlers, but her case led to a huge public trial. Standing there in the spotlight, she showed herself to be a jerk—not because she stole and branded a few cattle that weren't hers, but because her hatred for a large cattle baron led her to drive his cattle cruelly off cliffs and to marry his right-hand man in an attempt to ruin him.

Adjutant General John Chase and Lieutenant Karl Linderfeldt during the coal strike in Ludlow, and Captain Louis Scherf in the coal strike in Serene proved so bloodthirsty and callous in their handling of peaceful strikers that "jerk" is almost too kind a label for them.

Some of these men and women date back to fairly recent history. Others lived a long time ago and have achieved legend status. When faced with varying accounts of an incident or even flat-out contradictions, describing what happened during what circumstances, the author made a choice of what to believe based on what seemed reasonable or was best supported by evidence. When historians have a substantial disagreement, the author has noted this in the text.

Enjoy the escapades of these famous figures. It is possible and appropriate to applaud their achievements while deploring their moments of jerkdom.

CHAPTER 1

John C. Frémont
and Bill Williams

A THIRD OF THE MEN LOST

*B*y most standards, the fourth expedition of John Charles Frémont in 1848–49 was a disaster. It is true that, as Frémont complained afterwards, the failure can largely be blamed on the fact that Kit Carson, who had been Frémont's guide on earlier trips, was unavailable to lead this new expedition. But it was not just the lack of a good guide that contributed to the trip's failure. Many of the men who signed on were inexperienced; the journey started out late in the fall, which meant going into the mountains of southern Colorado during early heavy snows; and at many critical times during the trip, bad choices were made. In fact, historians—with the clarity that comes only in hindsight—have wondered how in one trip both the guide, Bill Williams, and the expedition leader, John C. Frémont, could have made so many wrong decisions with respect to timing, routes taken, and the men selected for specific tasks.

After allowing Williams to strand his men in the San Juan Mountains, Frémont continued to make bad choices that further jeopardized the lives of his men. Fremont did not return himself but sent others into the mountains to save his men. Then he risked more lives by sending men back just to rescue abandoned equipment. Although he had a terrible guide who can rightly be blamed for his part in this disastrous expedition, John C. Frémont's selfish disregard for the safety of his men showed him to be the real jerk.

It was Christmas Day, 1849, in the snowy San Juan Mountains of southern Colorado. John Charles Frémont and his expedition-

John Charles Frémont
COURTESY COLORADO HISTORICAL SOCIETY

ary group had failed to find a westward route off the mountain they had foolishly labored to climb. Food supplies were dangerously low; pack animals were dying of starvation and exhaustion. Around the fire that night, the men ate the butchered carcass of one of their mules. Other exhausted and starving pack animals lay dying not far off in the deep snow. The weary men called it Camp Dismal.

Frémont's guide had made a series of terrible decisions. Either he had lied about his knowledge of the area, had forgotten his way, or was deliberately leading them to failure. As a result, the men found themselves in desperate straits. A small rescue party was organized. Four men would go and try to find their way to a New Mexico settlement to buy food and mules and then come back to save the others. The rescue mission should take no more than a week, they thought. Although it would be difficult, the other men could hang on for that long. Yet who did Frémont include in the four-man rescue group? Bill Williams, the very guide who was responsible for getting them into this terrible predicament in the first place.

One agonizingly slow week passed and then another, as the starving and freezing men awaited the return of their comrades with mules and supplies. Clearly something had gone terribly wrong with the rescue party. Frémont selected another small group of men to join him in a second rescue attempt. Was it too late? Had the successful young army man, John Charles Frémont, totally failed his men and his mission?

John Charles Frémont was born on January 21, 1813, in Savannah, Georgia. His father, Charles Fremon, had immigrated to America from France. His beautiful mother was the subject of much gossip in Richmond, Virginia, for leaving her elderly husband to run off with her young French lover. Although a petition for divorce was filed, there is no evidence that it was ever granted. In polite Savannah society, John Charles Frémont—who at some point added the letter "t" to his surname—was viewed as being an illegitimate child.

Frémont attended school, majoring in science, at the College of Charleston. In 1831, just three months short of graduation, he was dismissed for "incorrigible negligence." Through the influence of family friends, Frémont was given a civilian post as a teacher of mathematics to midshipmen on the USS *Natchez*. During 1836 and 1837 he assisted in a survey for the Charleston and Cincinnati Railroad. In 1838, due to the influence of his friend, Secretary of War Joel Poinsett of South Carolina, Frémont was commissioned a second lieutenant in the United States Corps of Topographical Engineers.

Frémont accompanied a French scientist named Joseph Nicollet on field exploration trips to Minnesota. From Nicollet, Frémont not only learned the nuts and bolts of managing an expedition, but he picked up at least a rudimentary knowledge of geology. He also learned how to make astronomical observations and to use a barometer to measure altitude. In addition, Frémont acquired some basic knowledge of plants from the botanist who was part of the Nicollet expedition.

After these explorations Frémont spent some time in Washington, D.C. There he met seventeen-year-old Jessie, the daughter of Senator Thomas Benton. The two eloped. His powerful father-in-law, and the senator's equally powerful and wealthy friends, would prove from that point onward to be a big asset to Frémont's career.

In the spring of 1842, Frémont led his own expedition to explore the Platte River. He took with him a crew of skilled men guided by the capable and resourceful Kit Carson. This trip was successful, and the next year, he was sent out on another survey assignment. Frémont's wife helped him write lively reports of his expeditions, and his cartographer, Charles Preuss, drew maps that gave an accurate picture of the West. These two contributed greatly to the value and general acceptance of Frémont's work. After the reports and maps were published by Congress and in commercial editions, Frémont became a sort of national hero.

He was made a captain and in 1845 went off on another expedition. This time he was sent to California and soon was commissioned a lieutenant colonel in the Mounted Rifles. In California he became involved in what would be known as the Bear Flag Rebellion against Mexico. The chief of the naval and land operations on the Pacific Coast, Robert Stockton, appointed Frémont governor of the territory. When General Stephen Kearny arrived on the scene, however, a power struggle ensued between Admiral Stockton and General Kearny. Frémont chose to back Stockton and found himself in a poor position when General Kearny prevailed.

Because his actions in California appeared insubordinate to General Kearny, Frémont was court-martialed and convicted of mutiny and disobedience. Through Frémont's powerful Washington connections, President James Polk himself was persuaded to step in. The president used his authority to remit the penalty and order Frémont back to duty again. Frémont's pride had suffered, and he was angry at the treatment he had received. He chose to quit the army, planning to settle as a civilian with his wife in California.

But first Frémont wanted to make another expedition. No doubt his zeal for this task was partly to regain his former fame and stature and perhaps partly because he genuinely wanted to gather additional scientific and geological information. After the court-martial, however, even his powerful father-in-law was not able to convince Congress to fund another Frémont expedition. He was, however, able to find some wealthy St. Louis businessmen who were willing to fund a different kind of expedition. This one would seek a more satisfactory southerly railroad route across the United States close to the thirty-eighth parallel, which crosses the San Luis Valley of Colorado near Crestone.

Some veterans from Frémont's other expeditions signed on with him in this new adventure. Included in the party were a physician, a millwright, a gunsmith, and Frémont's favorite cartographer, Charles Pruess. Some of the others in the group were gentlemen who were willing to pay their own way to make the journey. Some of these gentlemen were artists, and although they were intrigued with the idea of the journey, they were not interested in doing any sort of hard labor on the trip. This, of course, would be a liability and a contentious issue once the journey was well underway. This expeditionary party was far different in its make-up from the experienced voyageurs, trappers, and military men with whom Frémont had traveled before. In fact, many of the men were totally inexperienced in survival techniques.

It was October 3, 1848, when John C. Frémont left St. Louis with thirty-five men on his fourth major expedition, bound for California. They crossed Kansas and reached Chouteau's Island on the Arkansas River by November 8, 1848. They followed the Arkansas to Big Timbers (close to what is now Lamar, Colorado) where many Native Americans were camped. The Native Americans warned Frémont that there were early, deep snows in the mountains. Some expeditionary leaders, especially those concerned for the welfare of their men, might have heeded this advice, but Frémont chose to ignore it.

By November 17, Frémont and his men were camped close to Bent's Fort, having traveled well-known trails to this point. From the fort Frémont wrote a letter to his father-in-law, Senator Benton, in which he acknowledged the bad weather he was facing. He wrote, "Both Indians and whites here report the snow to be deeper in the mountains than has for a long time been known so early in the season and they predict a severe winter. This morning, for the first time, the mountains showed themselves covered with snow, as well as the country around us; for it has snowed steadily and for the greater part of yesterday and the night before. They look imposing and somewhat stern; still I am in no wise discouraged and believe that we shall succeed in forcing our way across."

On his earlier journeys to Oregon and California, Frémont had used Kit Carson and Thomas Fitzpatrick as guides. But this time when the fully equipped Frémont prepared to leave from Bent's Fort to head into unfamiliar territory, he still had not secured the services of a guide. When Frémont learned that Kit Carson was not available, he and his men left the fort, planning to pick up a guide along the way.

The small expeditionary group set up camp among some cottonwoods on November 22, not far from El Pueblo de San Carlos. By chance, William Shirley Williams was at the old pueblo at this time. He came to them and offered to serve as their guide. Bill Williams had a lot of experience in the mountains, and Frémont hired him.

Williams was sixty-one years old. He had been a parson in his younger years, but he had given up the ministry long ago and had trapped all over the West with the well-known mountain man Jedediah Smith. Williams had the reputation of being something of a scoundrel and not the most trustworthy of men, but Frémont either did not know this or was simply desperate for a guide.

Some historians, dumbfounded by the poor choices Bill Williams made for the Frémont expedition, have suggested that Williams might have deliberately led the men astray, hoping to cause their deaths and make profits from selling the equipment that the men carried with them. While that is a possibility, the fact that Williams himself came close to perishing while on his rescue mission supports another view: that Williams really did not know this particular area very well and became confused and lost in the heavy snow.

Guided by Williams, the group set out on their journey. They crossed the Arkansas River several times and passed near what is presently Florence, Colorado. Williams led them over hills and valleys. The Wet Mountains were to the north of them as they approached the valley of the Huerfano River. In the deep, early snow the men moved more slowly than originally planned and used up more of their supplies than expected. At this point, seeing the heavy snow and the drain on supplies, and knowing that he didn't have the best of guides, Frémont made yet another poor decision: In spite of the weather, he chose to continue.

The group followed a wagon road along the north side of the river and continued through a canyon and over the hills. Although it was windy, there was less snow there. On December 3 they reached the 9,175-foot summit of Mosca Pass, where they looked down into the San Luis Valley. This route over Mosca Pass had taken a week and further depleted their supplies. A different route would have been more efficient, but for reasons unknown, Bill Williams did not select the easier route. They continued down the road and made camp at what is now Great Sand Dunes National Monument. It was about seventeen degrees below zero.

The next day they tried to find their way between the sand hills and the mountains, but made little progress through the snow and suffered from the extreme cold and wind. After three days, when even the noon temperatures were below zero, the expedition finally succeeded in going over the crest of the sand hills in snow six feet deep. By the time they reached the shelter of some trees north of the dunes, the men had icicles hanging from their beards and hair. They gathered leaves from the ground beneath the trees and put them under their bedding to try to protect themselves from the freezing temperatures.

They proceeded west-northwest toward the Rio Grande River and the San Juan Mountains. Apparently Frémont wanted to continue toward the Saguache Valley, but Williams said they could make up the time they had already lost by instead using Carnero Creek. Actually if the men had taken either the Saguache route or the Carnero Creek route, they probably would have been all right and well on their way to California. Instead, the men let Bill Williams lead the way. He soon became lost so that the men found themselves high above their destination on the ridges of Mesa Mountain. Historians who have retraced the trip believe that when faced with a choice, Bill Williams chose the worst possible route every time.

Charles Preuss, the cartographer for the group, kept a diary of the trip, which has proved very helpful to historians. In his notes, Preuss pointed out that Williams did not seem very familiar with the area. In fact, he wrote that they missed the pass they were searching for and had to make a wide detour. More snow fell, hampering the progress of the men and their 120 mules. When they finally arrived at La Garrita Creek, Preuss noted, "It was obvious that Bill had never been here." If this was obvious to the cartographer, it must also have been obvious to Frémont.

Again it appears that, as leader of the expedition and in the face of accumulating evidence that their guide did not know the area, Frémont had a choice. The men could have descended and worked their way back toward the routes that led to Carnero or Cochetopa Passes, or they could continue to work their way to the summit of Mesa Mountain. Frémont chose to believe Bill Williams, who said once they crossed this mountain they would find a snow-free tableland that would lead them to the Great Basin, and from there to California.

Even though experienced men in the expedition had many doubts about Williams's knowledge of the area, Frémont chose to take the old guide's advice and continued to lead his men and his nearly exhausted baggage-laden mules into the mountains. The mules stumbled over rocks and foundered in snow that in some places lay fifteen feet deep. According to diary accounts, on December 13 it took them an hour and a half to move forward three hundred feet. Still they continued to struggle onward. The men made camp a quarter of a mile below the summit of 12,944-foot Mesa Mountain.

One of the men wrote in his diary that the last two days had been a terrible ordeal. He said that the snow was "elbow deep when mounted on mules." Eight of their pack animals had been lost. On December 16, they tried to follow the ridge of the mountain to the top with some men going ahead to try to break a trail using wood from tree trunks to cut a channel in the snow. The temperature was twenty below zero. Many of the mules were gasping and collapsing. Some appeared to be so stressed by hunger and exhaustion that they became crazed and rushed from the trail, plunging over the edge.

The next day they again had the opportunity to work their way down and back to one of the two passes, but instead they continued to head upwards to the summit, apparently still believing Williams's promise of a "snow-free tableland." A blizzard hit and stopped them for several days on the mountain. Most of the remaining mules died of starvation. On December 22, after failing to find a westward trail off the mountain, Frémont and his men made camp on the southern slope.

By now, the snow, cold, difficult terrain, and scarcity of food had made the men desperate. Frémont decided to send a party of four, including Henry King as leader and Bill Williams as guide, to the nearest Spanish town, which Williams thought was Abiqui. (He was wrong, of course.) There they would buy animals and food to bring back to the others. Frémont gave King $1,800 to pay for the supplies.

The rest of the men tried building sleds to carry their equipment to the next campsite, but this effort was a failure. Only a few of their animals were alive by this time, and the men were eating the dead mules. Morale, however, had improved because the men thought that surely the rescuers would return within the week with supplies. The remainder of the group continued to move forward. Because they tried to drag their equipment with them, the men were unable to follow the route that the rescue group had taken. Although they could move only about three miles a day from camp to camp, the men continued forward in the hope that the rescue party would soon return.

The men established a cache called "Colonel's Camp" that could easily be identified by a large rock outcropping. It was here that they dragged heavy bundles and baggage to be left until the rescuers returned with fresh mules. By now, animosity was building in the group. While most of the men labored to drag equipment through the snow, some of the "gentlemen" who had signed on for the trip believed themselves to be exempt from any sort of labor. They let the others struggle while they passed their time in reading, writing, and playing the flute.

Increasingly the men found it difficult to think of themselves as one cohesive and supportive unit. The party broke into three groups, based primarily on friendships, to move slowly forward, carrying their own supplies and scavenging for food. Within a few days, one of these small groups had dropped about three miles behind the others. On January 9, one of the veteran members of the expedition died of exhaustion and cold. At this point, having waited for the return of the first rescue party for many days, Frémont decided that they must have met with some sort of disaster such as being killed by hostile Indians. He decided to take four men and lead another attempt to reach the New Mexican settlements. The others were to finish transporting the baggage to the cache and then to follow.

Actually, the original rescue party was not far ahead of Frémont. They had made very slow progress in their attempt to reach a village. Williams had urged the group to leave the Rio Grande River and cross the sagebrush prairie. Once again, their guide had led them astray. Their feet and fingers became frozen and some of the men were snow-blind. Hopelessly lost fifteen days after having set out on their rescue mission, they had used up all their provisions and even eaten leather to ward off starvation. In his notes, Andrew Cathcart wrote about "living on hide, rope, and leather for weeks, and then no food for days." King, the leader of the small rescue group, became delirious, fell behind, and died. Some evidence suggests that the remaining men may have resorted to cannibalism to stay alive. Cathcart writes, "Some of the survivors fed on dead bodies of comrades. I saw some awful scenes."

Frémont and his small rescue party came across an Indian and managed to converse with him in Spanish. He took them to his lodging, fed them, and led them to a small settlement on the Rio Colorado where they were able to get some horses and food. Frémont was continuing toward some larger settlements when he noticed a plume of smoke near a grove of trees. He proceeded there and found the three surviving members of the first rescue party. Earlier that day, almost miraculously, one of the men saw and shot a deer. The starving men, including Bill Williams the guide, were eating it around a campfire when Frémont and his group met up with them.

The second rescue party, traveling only four days, had caught up with the original rescue party that had started out twenty-two days earlier. Putting the three emaciated men from the first party on horses, the combined group headed toward other settlements near present-day Questa, New Mexico. They reached a small village that had no mules, only goats. Women in the village baked bread and gathered supplies for them to take to the lost men, while one of Frémont's party, Alexander Godey, rode thirteen miles to another larger settlement to buy thirty mules and a hog.

Now that they had found supplies, Frémont made another decision that branded him a jerk. Instead of going back to rescue his men, Frémont went on to Taos to recuperate at the home of Kit Carson. He chose Godey to go back with four Indians, the mules, and supplies to try to rescue the others who had been left stranded in the San Juan Mountains. Frémont left another of his men, Charles Pruess, at the Rio Colorado to wait for Godey and the others. In a letter to his wife written in Taos on January 27, 1849, Frémont justifies his choice by writing, "I remain here with old comrades, while Godey goes back; because it was not necessary for me to go with him."

In this same letter, Frémont lays the blame for his expedition's failure squarely upon Bill Williams. He writes, "At Pueblo, I had engaged as a guide an old trapper, known as Bill Williams, and who had spent some twenty-five years of his life in trapping in various parts of the Rocky Mountains. The error of our expedition was committed in engaging this man. He proved never to have known, or entirely to have forgotten, the whole country through which we were to pass." Nowhere in the letter does Frémont take any responsibility for his contributions to the disastrous trip. Nor does he appear to be in the least disturbed about sitting and writing in comfort not knowing what had happened to the men he was supposedly leading.

Eighteen miles above the mouth of the Conejos, Godey and his team found the first of the abandoned men. Seven of those in this small group had already died. Continuing north, Godey's rescue crew found another small group. Two of the men in this group had died. A final man straggling behind was found. Godey and his crew made it back again to the settlement with the survivors and some baggage and Frémont's trunk. One of the survivors, Andrew Cathcart, wrote a letter on February 10, 1849, describing his ordeal in the mountains and his present condition. "I am a perfect skeleton, snow-blind, frostbitten, and hardly able to stand."

On February 12, two months after they started into the San Juan Mountains, Frémont, Charles Pruess, Alexander Godey, Bill Williams, and the eighteen other survivors of the expedition were reunited in Taos. Unfortunately, two more losses were yet to come.

When this expedition had started out in St. Louis, they carried some valuable pieces of equipment including a chronometer, a sextant, compasses, a refractory telescope, and a two-foot telescope on a transit. Determined not to lose his equipment, even though he had lost more than a third of his men, Frémont sent two of his men back to rescue it. Frémont was willing to risk the loss of his men rather than lose his instruments. On their journey to the cache, Frémont's two men, including Bill Williams, were in fact met and killed by hostile Indians. The equipment was never recovered. Frémont finally did reach California, using a southern route suggested by Kit Carson.

John C. Frémont never finished his report of the fourth expedition. The tale of freezing cold, exhaustion, starvation, hints of cannibalism, and lack of leadership was no doubt a bitter disappointment that Frémont in no way wanted to immortalize in writing. For the failure of the expedition, it is fair to blame Bill Williams. If, as some think, he deliberately led the men astray, planning to let them die and come back to gather and profit from the abandoned equipment, he was certainly a jerk. But Frémont, in his lack of leadership, his failure to take part in the rescue of his men, and his willingness to send two more men to their deaths in another attempt to retrieve his equipment, also behaved like a jerk. And perhaps worst of all, he never took responsibility for his own contributions to the failure of the fourth expedition.

SOURCES

Richmond, Patricia Joy. *Trail to Disaster.* Denver, CO: Colorado Historical Society, 1990. The author made numerous trips into the area where Frémont and his men were lost and writes in great detail about it.

Simmons, Virginia McConnell. *The San Luis Valley: Land of the Six Armed Cross,* 2nd ed. Niwot, CO: University of Colorado Press, 1999. Provides a general history of the San Luis Valley.

Spence, Mary Lee, ed. *The Expeditions of John Charles Frémont, Vol. 3, Travels from 1848–1854.* Chicago: University of Chicago Press, 1984. This is one of a series of volumes about Frémont's expeditions and includes maps and letters.

Wheeler, Richard S. *Snowbound.* New York: Tom Doherty Associates, 2010. A biographical novel giving a fictional first-person account of Frémont after his failed expedition.

CHAPTER 2

Colonel John M. Chivington

THE SAND CREEK MASSACRE

*T*he Sand Creek Massacre, which took place in the southeastern Colorado Territory in 1864, is one of the most controversial historical battles involving Native Americans in our country's history. Some say no massacre occurred; they call this the Battle of Sand Creek. Others insist that the fault was entirely due to Colonel John M. Chivington and they call it the Chivington Massacre. Either way, when the battle was over, mutilated bodies of more than one hundred Native Americans lay on the field.

Immediately after the event, there were inquiries and investigations by both the army and Congress, and the topic was debated in newspaper editorials all over the country. Historians agree that the Sand Creek Massacre was not part of a governmental policy. General Samuel Curtis gave what can best be called vague orders, and the actual attack was under the direct command of Colonel John M. Chivington. Unbiased accounts are scarce, and there are many defenders of Chivington, but the recorded testimony given by a variety of men who were at Sand Creek suggests that in his involvement at the Sand Creek Massacre, Colonel Chivington behaved like a jerk.

It was quiet in the first light of November 19, 1864. Black Kettle's Cheyenne camped in a village located in a bend of the dry-bedded Sand Creek amidst a few cottonwood and willow trees in the southeastern Colorado Territory. Nearby, a herd of horses was grazing. Southward, not far from the Cheyenne, were the lodges of the Arapaho under the leadership of Chief Left Hand. In the cool early morning air, a few people in camp had just started to stir. Then a cloud of dust appeared—not a herd of buffalo, but the approach of soldiers, shouting and firing guns.

Colonel John M. Chivington

Counting on the element of surprise for his attack, Colonel John Chivington had arrived at Sand Creek near the encampment of the Cheyenne and Arapaho when most people in the camp were still asleep. First Chivington sent three companies to charge across the creek and cut the village off from its herd of horses. Another group of men was sent to capture another herd of horses that was southwest of the village. Other men took up their positions and waited for Chivington, who halted his men in the bed of the river below the village.

Chivington gave the rallying cry to his men to "Remember the murdered women and children on the Platte," referring to recent vicious attacks on white settlements made by marauding Indians. His men began firing into Black Kettle's village, which quickly erupted in panic.

As the shouting and firing continued, Chief Black Kettle took a large American garrison flag that had been given to him some years earlier and raised it on a lodgepole with a white flag flapping underneath it. He called out to the soldiers that the camp was friendly, and he urged his own people not to be afraid.

Other accounts of that day state that White Antelope, another old Cheyenne chief, also ran toward the soldiers, yelling at the troops not to fire. He finally stopped and folded his arms over his chest, showing that the Native Americans had no desire to fight. The soldiers kept coming and shot White Antelope where he stood. Chivington was witness to these actions, yet he took no move to stop the firing and simply capture this group that was offering no resistance.

Only a few days earlier, unknown to Chivington, Major Scott Anthony at Fort Lyon had sent John Smith and Private David Louderback to Sand Creek to determine how many Native Americans were there and whether they were friendly to the whites or not. Another man accompanied them to trade goods with the Indians. These three visitors were in Black Kettle's camp when Chivington's attack began. Unable to get to a horse, Smith, carrying a white flag, walked out of his tent, hoping to talk to the soldiers and find out what they wanted. Since he was dressed in a hat, overcoat, and trousers, he did not think he would be mistaken for an Indian. But when he got close to the troops, the soldiers fired on him, so he quickly retreated back to camp.

Army Private Louderback finally managed to get the attention of Colonel Chivington, who halted the shooting long enough to allow the private and the other visiting white men to fall into the back of the command. Had he taken a moment to listen to the private, Chivington would have learned that this was a friendly group, but immediately Chivington and his men commenced shooting again. Chief Left Hand's camp, in the middle of the lodges, was hit especially hard.

Accounts differ as to the number of men involved on the battlefield. Best estimates seem to be between six hundred and a thousand soldiers. There were about five to six hundred Native Americans in the camps of Black Kettle and Left Hand. Most of the Indian men were out hunting. Of those in camp, about 130 were warriors and the rest were women and children. By the end of the day, many would be slaughtered.

Some of the Cheyenne tried to escape by moving up the creek bed. They sought a place where they could dig holes in the bank for some protection. Using bows, they shot back at their attackers. A few soldiers were killed by their arrows, while many of these Native American men, women, and children were shot by the soldiers. Captain Silas Soule and his men were part of the attacking force. Captain Soule was opposed to killing the peaceful Indians, so throughout the attack, he kept his squadron together but refused to order his men to fire. Apparently this did not cause Chivington to reconsider his own actions.

By three o'clock in the afternoon, the battle was over. A few Cheyenne and Arapaho had escaped, and some soldiers pursued them. The majority of the soldiers then returned to the camp where they attempted to identify the chiefs who had been killed. They looted and took souvenirs: jewelry, scalps, and body parts. No prisoners were taken. Chivington did nothing to try to spare a single life. There is no evidence that Colonel Chivington in any way tried to restrain his troops from these savage acts. He may not have been able to control these relatively untrained and undisciplined men even if he had tried; but he did not try.

That night Chivington wrote a dispatch to General Curtis in which he listed the army casualties as nine killed and thirty-eight wounded. He gave the exaggerated figure that between four hundred and five hundred Indians were killed, including Chiefs Black Kettle and White Antelope.

In other reports, Chief Left Hand was also listed as killed. Although some historians insist that Chief Left Hand escaped, Margaret Coel's extensive research indicates that in fact he died at Sand Creek. Later reports show that Black Kettle did escape. In fact, on October 13, 1865, Black Kettle was one of those who signed the Treaty of the Little Arkansas River at Bluff Creek. Black Kettle was finally killed on November 27, 1868, at a Cheyenne camp on the banks of the Washita River in Indian Territory by General Custer's Seventh Cavalry.

Colonel Chivington also sent a letter the night after the battle to the editor of the Denver newspaper, the *Rocky Mountain News*, telling about his victory in "one of the most bloody Indian battles ever fought on these plains." Historians believe that the number of dead Native Americans was probably considerably less than the number reported by Chivington.

The next morning Chivington led his men southward toward the Arkansas hoping to find another band of Arapaho led by Little Raven. Chivington camped about fifteen miles from the battlefield and sent the army dead and wounded back to Fort Lyon. For the next several days, his soldiers hunted the elusive Indians, but only found their empty camps each day. Because his men and horses were tired, Chivington finally gave up his chase and started back to Fort Lyon on December 7, arriving there on December 10.

After the massacre at Sand Creek, the citizens of Denver welcomed the troops into town like conquering heroes. The *Rocky Mountain News* wrote in headlines, "Colorado Soldiers Have

Again Covered Themselves with Glory." Only after investigations began and testimony was heard and recorded about the brutality, scalping, and mutilations to warriors, women, and children, did the public finally realize this had not been a noble battle, but a massacre. Samuel G. Colley, an Indian agent who visited the battlefield, testified, "I saw the bodies of those lying there cut all to pieces, worse mutilated than any I ever saw before."

Although he was never officially punished for his role at Sand Creek, Chivington was forced to resign from the Colorado militia. Largely because of his involvement in what was proving to be a scandal, Colorado's Territorial Governor John Evans was removed from office in August 1865 by President Andrew Johnson.

How did it happen that a family man who neither cursed nor drank, who had been a national hero for his command at La Glorieta Pass, and who had preached the gospel to so many, commanded the troops at the massacre at Sand Creek? Who was Colonel John M. Chivington and what series of events had brought him to this time and place?

John Milton Chivington was born in a log cabin in Warren County, Ohio, on January 27, 1823. His father and brothers were large men, and John Chivington also grew to be well over six feet tall. He attended school when he could, but he was mostly taught by his mother. When Chivington was thirteen, he joined his older brother in a timber business, and at eighteen he took over the business. He made frequent raft trips with the timber to Cincinnati. In 1840 he met and married Martha Rollason. To better support his wife, Chivington apprenticed himself to a carpenter and learned the trade.

In 1842 Chivington attended several revival meetings held by an evangelist. He joined the Methodist Church, and soon after decided he wanted to enter the ministry. He could not afford to abandon his job and spend time in a seminary, but with the help of an encouraging bishop, he borrowed books and schooled himself at home. Once ordained, in September 1844, he was put in charge of the Zoar Church in the Goshen circuit of the Ohio Conference.

After that, Chivington took on a number of assignments, each for two years, in which he helped establish churches and build congregations, and contributed in the communities in which he lived by helping to build strong schools and libraries. In 1848 he moved to Quincy, Illinois, and took on new assignments in the Illinois Conference of the Methodist-Episcopal Church. During this time, he became an ardent and outspoken foe of slavery. He was also sent into Indian country to serve as a missionary to the Wyandot Indians, where he built a log church and preached to them through an interpreter.

His next assignment in 1854 took him to St. Joseph, Missouri, during border warfare between Kansas and Missouri. Chivington remained a stout opponent of slavery. He was next sent to Nebraska City to help organize the local district church. In all of his church assignments, Chivington was very successful. In March 1860 he was appointed Elder of the Rocky Mountain District. He set out with his family on the Overland Trail to Fort Kearney and then on to Denver.

Once in Denver, Chivington built a house and began to organize his new church district. He not only preached in Denver but in mining towns from Central City to Georgia Gulch. Chivington became respected throughout the territory for his preaching and for his activities in communities through improving schools. He also became known for his leadership and involvement in the Masonic Lodge. He made friends and became acquainted with the powerful leaders of Denver.

Because of his strong feelings against slavery, Chivington was concerned when the news of the secession of South Carolina reached the Colorado Territory. At the outbreak of the Civil War, the governor of the Colorado Territory, William Gilpin, offered Chivington a position as an army chaplain. Chivington turned down this offer, asking for a "fighting" position instead. He joined the First Colorado regiment as a major.

It wasn't long before Chivington found himself at La Glorieta Pass in eastern New Mexico. It was 1862, a critical moment when it looked as if the Confederates might convince the West to support their side of the war. At first, the battle between the Union soldiers and the Confederates appeared to be an impossible fight. Outnumbered more than four to one, the Colorado and New Mexico volunteers put up a good fight against the Confederates, but the outcome was certainly in doubt. Then Chivington came to the rescue.

Through a series of successful maneuvers, Chivington and about four hundred of his men got behind enemy lines. Chivington led his troops in a surprise attack on the Confederate supply train. His soldiers rappelled down canyon walls, taking the small group of men guarding the supplies by surprise and capturing the entire Confederate supply train of eighty wagons, including quartermaster stores and ordnance supplies. Since he couldn't safely transport these, Chivington blew up all the supplies and supervised the bayoneting of five hundred to six hundred draft and riding animals. Without supplies, the Confederates were forced to abandon their plans to capture Colorado and the West. Chivington returned to Colorado a hero.

As the huge influx of people swept in with the gold rush, more and more energy was directed into moving Colorado from a territory to statehood. John Evans became the second territorial governor. The newly organized Republican Party took notice of this army hero and began grooming Chivington for a life in politics. He appeared to be a likely candidate as the new state's first member of Congress.

With the Civil War and statehood occupying center stage, few paid attention to what was happening with the Native American population in the Colorado Territory. People like William Bent tried to point out that the Native Americans were restless and unhappy with the increasing number of whites on what they regarded as their land. Prospectors and farmers were laying claim to land that by treaty had already been given to Native Americans. Although older tribesmen still wanted peace, an increasing number of the younger Native Americans seemed willing to raise war to drive the white men out. Bent shared his thoughts with the Bureau of Indian Affairs, but he was largely ignored.

In February 1862, when the First Colorado Regiment had marched south to fight in the Civil War, no troops were left in the Colorado Territory to protect homesteaders from hostile Indians. Raids by Native Americans increased. A second regiment of Colorado volunteers was organized in May.

When Chivington returned from his fighting at La Glorieta Pass, he was made Commander of the Military District of Colorado. It was an uneasy time. Incidents of hostility on both sides were common occurrences. Indians were attacking small settlements, killing, and stealing. Soldiers were burning Indian camps. Rumors arose that there might be a combined attack of various Indian tribes on whites the following spring.

At the same time, discussion raged in Denver's newspapers about the dangers posed to the white population by Native Americans. Papers went so far as to advocate on front pages for the "extermination of the red devils." This sentiment led Colorado Territorial Governor Evans to present and support new efforts to control the Native Americans.

Colonel Chivington formed the Third Cavalry, a volunteer unit of about one thousand men. Many of the volunteers came from mining camps and Denver saloons. Most of these men had no military training but were eager to help Chivington in what they thought would be action to "burn villages and kill Cheyenne." They signed up for one hundred days of service.

Receiving directions from Washington, Governor Evans tried to organize meetings with the Cheyenne and Arapaho to negotiate treaties, but the Native Americans did not attend. In June, a rider came into Denver telling of an Arapaho attack involving the massacre of an entire family and the ranch foreman at Running Creek, leaving bodies scalped and mutilated. Fear and anger against the Native Americans ran high.

In spite of the recent violence, Governor Evans again tried to take a step toward peace, sending messages to the Indians of the

Plains in June 1864, directing all friendly tribesmen to report to Forts Lyon, Larned, and Laramie and Camp Collins, where they would be safe. They were warned that Native Americans who did not report to these forts would be considered hostile, pursued, and destroyed.

In August, when no response came to the message, a public proclamation was made authorizing the pursuit and killing of all hostile Native Americans who had not reported to one of these forts or camps. Finally, in late August, Black Kettle sent a note to Fort Lyon offering to make peace. At the time he sent the letter, Black Kettle was camped at Smoky Hill River. Major Edward Wynkoop from Fort Lyon, who was well known for his fair dealings with Native Americans, rode to Smoky Hill to negotiate. There, acting in good faith, Black Kettle turned over some white prisoners, and Major Wynkoop made arrangements to have Black Kettle accompany him to Denver to meet with the governor and discuss peace.

Colonel Chivington was among those the governor brought with him to meet with Major Wynkoop and Black Kettle. Chief Left Hand's brother attended the meeting while a subchief represented Left Hand. Chivington insisted on terms that included complete surrender. The Native Americans were to bring their bands to the vicinity of Fort Lyon and surrender their weapons.

Following this meeting, in mid-October, Chief Left Hand brought his band of Arapaho to Fort Lyon and surrendered. Chief Little Raven also came with his people. They turned over their few weapons and relied upon the army fort to feed them. Because Colonel Chivington and others thought Wynkoop was too sympathetic to Native Americans, he was rather suddenly removed from his post, and Major Scott Anthony took over at Fort Lyon.

Black Kettle and his Cheyenne were devoted to Wynkoop, but were distrustful of Major Scott Anthony. Chief Black Kettle and Chief War Bonnet rode to Fort Lyon with about sixty men. Major Anthony met them outside the fort and said he lacked authority to conclude a peace treaty and would not permit them to stay near the post. He did not want the expense and responsibility for feeding all these Indians, and he did not like the danger posed by their large numbers so close to his fort.

Major Anthony told the Cheyenne that they might safely camp on Sand Creek and would be under the protection of Fort Lyon while they were there. Major Anthony also told Chief Left Hand that his Arapaho should take back the arms they had surrendered, leave the post, and go hunt to support themselves, stating that he could no longer supply them with rations.

Little Raven distrusted Major Anthony. He decided to move his people farther away down the Arkansas and most of the Arapaho went with him. Chief Left Hand took a small group of his people and went to Sand Creek, only about thirty-five miles away, to make camp with Black Kettle and his Cheyenne.

Meanwhile, Chivington and several companies of men had assembled at Camp Evans. Many of these men who had signed on for only one hundred days of service were disappointed at not having seen any action against Native Americans. They moved toward Denver where General Patrick Connor paid a visit. Colonel Chivington believed General Connor had been sent there to check on whether or not the campaign against hostile Indians was being carried out. Chivington promised to keep the general advised of the results of any engagement.

On November 23, Colonel Chivington arrived at Camp Fillmore and assumed command of the expedition. The next morning the troops were on the road. They reached Fort Lyon just before noon on November 28. Steps were immediately taken to make sure no one could leave the fort and perhaps alert the Native Americans in the area to their presence. Such warnings were highly likely because many of the men in the fort regarded the Native Americans as friendly and did not perceive them as a threat.

Major Scott Anthony was delighted to see the troops. He reported to Chivington that there were Cheyenne and Arapaho at Sand Creek and more Cheyenne at Smoky Hills, and that all were hostile. In spite of Major Anthony's words, Chivington must have known that many of the other officers in the fort did not believe this to be the case. Colonel Chivington chose to believe the worst about the Native Americans and was eager to give his men the chance to fight and kill. This would provide him with a victory, information that he could pass on to General Connor. The Colonel announced that he and his men would march to Sand Creek that night. Early the next morning, the massacre at Sand Creek occurred and Chivington earned his place in history.

Although he was not formally punished, Chivington was forced to resign after the attack at Sand Creek. It was the end of his career in the army and of his hopes of becoming a major political figure. The following year, he moved to Nebraska and became a successful freight hauler. He moved again, first to California and then to Ohio, where he farmed for a while and was editor of a small newspaper. Eventually he returned to Denver and worked as a deputy sheriff until his death in 1892.

Well over a hundred years later, in the 1990s, Sand Creek again made headlines in Colorado. A Civil War monument had been built at Colorado's capitol in Denver in 1909. The bronze statue showing a Union soldier stands near the west entrance to the capitol. At the base of the statue are four tables that list all the battles of the Civil War and elsewhere, and lists the names of Colorado soldiers who died in each battle. Among the battles listed was the one at Sand Creek. No one questioned this for decades. Then someone both noticed and objected to the historical plaque. Believing it to be a massacre rather than a battle, many interested citizens, including descendents of Native Americans who were killed or wounded at Sand Creek, suddenly started speaking up. They argued that mention of this "battle" at Sand Creek should be removed from the plaque.

After a great deal of discussion and debate, it was finally decided to leave the statue and plaques as they were but to add a fifth table, which was authorized by Senate Joint Resolution 99-017. The fifth plaque reads:

The controversy surrounding this Civil War Monument has become a symbol of Coloradans' struggle to understand and take responsibility for our past. On November 29, 1864, Colorado's First and Third Cavalry, commanded by Colonel John Chivington, attacked Chief Black Kettle's peaceful camp of Cheyenne and Arapaho Indians on the banks of Sand Creek about 180 miles southeast of here. In the surprise attack, soldiers killed more than 150 of the villages' 500 inhabitants. Most of the victims were elderly men, women and children.

Though some civilians and military personnel immediately denounced the attack as a massacre, others claimed the village was a legitimate target. This Civil War monument, paid for from funds by the Pioneers' Association and State, was erected on July 24, 1909, to honor all Colorado Soldiers who had fought in battles in the Civil War and elsewhere. By designating Sand Creek a battle, the monument's designers mischaracterized the actual events. Protests led by some Sand Creek descendants and others throughout the twentieth century have led to the widespread recognition of the tragedy of the Sand Creek Massacre.

After the people of Colorado revisited and reexamined the events of Sand Creek, many thought that there should also be some recognition by the federal government. In October 1998, President Bill Clinton signed into law a bill calling for the National Park Service to verify the site of the Sand Creek battleground and preserve and manage it. This proved to be a difficult assignment because there was no agreement on the actual location of the site. Over the years, the creek had dried up, filled up, and changed its course many times. Banks caved in. Winds kept reshaping the land. Lots of people had opinions, but there wasn't agreement as to the location of the battlefield. A group was formed to determine its exact location.

Two reports proved most helpful in locating the historic site. Lieutenant Samuel Bonsall led a ten-man detachment to the site in 1868. He took coordinates, made a map, and kept a journal. He reported gathering up a wagonload of artifacts from the site. William Bent's son, George, who had an Arapaho mother, was camped at Sand Creek during the Chivington attack. Wounded in the hip, he escaped and survived. He provided many details of where and how the battle took place.

Once the determination of the location was complete, the designation of the historic site went forward. On Saturday, April 28, 2007, the Sand Creek National Historic Site was dedicated. This historic site is open to visitors from April 1 to December 1 each year. It consists of more than 1,400 acres acquired by the government from Cheyenne and Arapaho tribes.

Visitors to the historic site are reminded of the long ago events at Sand Creek, when Native American women, children, and old men were slaughtered while Colonel John Milton Chivington stood by and did nothing to prevent the killings and mutilations.

SOURCES

Coel, Margaret. *Chief Left Hand*. Norman, OK: University of Oklahoma Press, 1981. This book was named best nonfiction book of the year in 1981 by the National Federation of Press Women.

Craig, Reginald S. *The Fighting Parson: The Biography of Colonel John M. Chivington*. Tucson, AZ: Westernlore Press, 1994.

Donnel, James E. *The Military Career of John M. Chivington: A Thesis*. Laramie, WY: University of Wyoming, 1960.

Dunn, William R. *I Stand By Sand Creek*. Fort Collins, CO: Old Army Press, 1985. Gives a different point of view to what some call a massacre.

Floyd, E. Randall. *The Good, the Bad, and the Mad: Weird People in American History*. Augusta, GA: Harbor House, 1999.

Hoig, Stan. *The Sand Creek Massacre*. Normal, OK: University of Oklahoma Press, 1961.

Mendoza, Patricia M. *Song of Sorrow: Massacre at Sand Creek.* Denver, CO: Willow Wind Publishing Co., 1993.

Schott, Bob. *Blood at Sand Creek: The Massacre Revisited.* Caldwell, ID: Caxton Printers, 1994.

Wood, Richard E. *Here Lies Colorado: Fascinating Figures in Colorado History.* Helena, MT: Farcountry Press, 2005.

Windham Thomas Wyndham-Quin
COURTESY COLORADO HISTORICAL SOCIETY

CHAPTER 3

Windham Thomas
Wyndham-Quin

EXTRAORDINARY LAND GRAB AT ESTES PARK

*P*resident Abraham Lincoln signed the original Homestead Act
*into law on May 20, 1862. Under the Homestead Act, an appli-
cant could apply for freehold title to up to 160 acres of undeveloped
land outside the original thirteen colonies. The applicant needed
to be an American who had never taken up arms against the U.S.
government. Freed slaves were allowed to apply. There was a three-
step process: file an application, improve the land, and file for a
deed of title. The requirements for improvements on the land were
minimal. If the applicant ploughed even an eighth of an acre of
land or made some attempt to build a cabin, that amount of work
was sufficient. Claims for land were not evaluated. Witnesses could
simply submit an affidavit that the person had lived on the piece of
land for a sufficient time and had made improvements.*

*Windham Thomas Wyndham-Quin, the Earl of Dunraven, was
part of the peerage in Ireland. He in no way qualified to file for
land in the United States through the Homestead Act. He could,
however, buy the land from others whom he paid to file the claims
and turn over the land to him. Taking advantage of the Homestead
Act put Windham Thomas Wyndham-Quin, the 4th Earl of Dunraven, squarely into contention for jerk status.*

Like so many people in the late 1800s who hoped to carve out a
better life, German immigrant George I. Bodde headed into the
Colorado Territory and claimed a piece of land near what is now
Estes Park, Colorado. His property was close to land that the Earl
of Dunraven had already bought from other homesteaders. Since

the earl was notorious for not respecting the land claims of others, Bodde built a fence around his land to protect it from the earl's roaming cattle.

Bodde's plan to preserve his homesteaded land was not successful. As fast as he built his fences, the earl's men, led by his overseer, Theodore Whyte, tore them down, and the earl's cattle came tromping onto Bodde's land. Each fence repair met the same fate. Finally realizing there was little he could do about it and harboring deep resentment against the earl and his overseer, Bodde reluctantly sold out and decided to move away.

Before Bodde left, however, quite by chance he met Theodore Whyte near a stream crossing. Recognizing his enemy, Bodde was so enraged that he grabbed Whyte and threatened to drown him right there in the creek. At the last moment, good sense prevailed and Bodde released Whyte who suffered only a good dunking. Many men in the area who shared Bodde's frustration and dislike for the earl and his men heartily wished Whyte had been drowned.

Bodde was just one of many men who were sometimes called the "Pioneers of 1885." Some stuck it out in Estes Park, Colorado, but many others were driven off by the high-handed tactics of the Earl of Dunraven.

Windham Thomas Wyndham-Quin, the 4th Earl of Dunraven and Mountearl in the Peerage of Ireland and second Baron Kenry of the United Kingdom, Knight of the Order of St. Patrick and Companion of the Order of St. Michael and St. George, was a man of great privilege, but he did not simply sit back and take life easy as a gentleman.

The Earl of Dunraven studied in Paris and Rome and completed his education at Christ Church, Oxford. After school, he served as a lieutenant in a cavalry regiment. At twenty-six he became a war correspondent for a London newspaper, the *Daily Telegraph,* and covered the Abyssinian War. In 1870–71, he was a special correspondent during the Franco-Prussian War and reported on the siege of Paris. He wrote under the name of Viscount Adare. He was a member of the House of Lords of the British Empire.

The earl was active in matters of state in Ireland and served as chairman of a committee involving the Irish Land Conference of 1902–3. He owned 39,000 acres of land at his Adare Manor Estate in County Limerick, Ireland, and had four homes, including Dunraven Castle located in Glamorgan, Ireland. Although he was a land owner, writer, and politician, life was not all work for the earl. As a wealthy member of the peerage in Ireland he could afford to raise horses, race yachts, and hunt big game. Hunting was a particular passion, and in his leisure time he hunted wild game throughout the world. Any chance to hunt in a new area captured his attention. When he heard about excellent hunting in the American West, of course he wanted to try it out.

The Earl of Dunraven was not a complete stranger to the United States. In fact, he brought his bride to the east coast of the United States on their honeymoon in 1869 but stayed only briefly. He first came to the West to hunt in the autumn of 1871. The earl always brought with him friends and relatives. On this trip, he brought along his personal physician, George Henry Kingley. From Chicago they traveled the Union Pacific Railroad to North Platte where they were met by their two guides, Buffalo Bill Cody and Texas Jack. For a month, they hunted elk and buffalo along the North Platte and south along both Medicine and Red Willow Creeks.

The hunting party reached Denver in December 1872, where the earl met Theodore Whyte who originally was from Devonshire, England. The two became friends, and Whyte told the earl about the fabulous hunting available in Estes Park, Colorado, with its plentiful deer, elk, and bear.

The earl and some of his friends, including Sir William Cummings and the Earl of Fitzpatrick, came to Estes Park. In his book, *Canadian Nights*, Lord Dunraven wrote a description of his first view of the area:

> *On the left, the hillside rises steeply, crowned with a buttress of frowning rock. On the right a mountain of almost*

solid rock stands naked and savage. In front, beyond the Park, the main range of mountains rears itself, topped with snow, rent in great chasms, pierced by the gloomy heavily-timbered depths of black canyon. On the extreme left and in the distance Longs Peak towers above its fellows; and beneath you, in strange contrast with the barren foot-hills through which you have passed, and the savage stern grandeur of the range, lies the Park—undulating, grass-covered dotted with trees, peaceful and quiet, with a silver thread of water curving and twining through its midst.

The earl and his companions stayed with Griffith Evans, an early settler in the area who provided room and board to visitors and who was delighted to have such distinguished guests. In describing his accommodations in Estes Park, the earl pointed out that while there was not much "elegance," there was plenty of "comfort." Arriving there in winter in freezing cold temperatures, the earl was not at all discouraged or put off. Immediately he set out hunting.

The earl loved the area and returned in 1873 for another visit. He hunted deer, elk, and mountain sheep. In writing about his admiration for the Rocky Mountains, he noted, "The air is scented with the sweet-smelling sap of the pines, whose branches welcome many feathered visitors from southern climes; an occasional humming-bird whirrs among the shrubs, trout leap in the creeks, insects buzz in the air; all nature is active and vibrant with life."

Finding the area so much to his liking, the earl wasn't content just to visit and enjoy it. He wanted to own it. Some of his detractors said he wanted to become the "Earl of Estes." His dream was to buy up all the available land as his own private hunting preserve. Being such a wealthy man, he could certainly afford to do this, but the Homestead Act of 1862 prevented him from buying it. The act provided for the transfer of 160 acres of unoccupied public land to each homesteader on payment of a nominal fee after five years of residence. Homesteaders needed to be the head of a family or twenty-one years of age. Land could also be acquired after only six months of residence on payment of $1.25 per acre. For the earl, the catch was that the homesteader had to be a citizen, or in the process of becoming a citizen, of the United States.

Since the Earl of Dunraven did not meet the citizenship requirement, he sought a way around it. What followed was the biggest land grab ever attempted in the American West. First, the earl had the land surveyed. Then with the help of his friend, Theodore Whyte, as well as that of several Denver bankers and lawyers he had met, the earl set about acquiring land. Dunraven established a company called Estes Park Company, Ltd. Theodore Whyte, or his agents, would find men willing to stake 160-acre claims under the Homestead Act. Then the Estes Park Company would buy the land from the homesteaders at a nominal price.

Clearly this was a scheme to buy up land, not legitimate homesteading. Whyte and his men would hire drunks and drifters from Larimer Street in Denver or seek out-of-work ranch hands in need of some ready cash. The only requirement made on these men was willingness to sign their name to the homestead records.

These people who supposedly wanted to settle on the land would file petitions for a subdivision of land. Then a survey would be made and the land claimed. Once a claim was filed, Whyte would then pay $1.25 to the government for each acre. To further meet the conditions of the Homestead Act, "improvements" were required on the land. In many cases the improvements were nothing more than four logs, laid out in the pattern of a square, which was said to be the start of a cabin.

Often the men who signed claims as homesteaders for the land were paid ten to fifty dollars, though in some cases, the earl paid more. His plan was to try to file for all the land where there were springs or streams. This would give him control of all the water sources in the area. In some cases, records indicate that the earl bought the same land twice, and in other instances, because of an error in township numbers, the earl missed out on a piece of land.

For the most part, however, his plan to buy the entire area was moving ahead rapidly.

Between 1874 and 1880, by using this means of buying up homesteads from men who had never seen and had no interest in living on the land, the Earl of Dunraven bought up 8,200 acres of land, and controlled another 7,000 acres of land through ownership of streams and springs. Legitimate homesteaders deeply resented this land grab and were especially angry that his claims deliberately blocked access to water for the settlers' cattle. During this time of land acquisition, the earl made annual visits to Estes Park and brought large numbers of friends and relatives to enjoy the hunting with him.

The earl became a cattle man of sorts, too. In addition to hunting, he decided to use some of his newly acquired land as a vast cattle ranch. Whyte imported from abroad some prize Herefords, registered a brand, and put the cattle on the earl's land. He put up fences and didn't seem to care if these fences crossed roads or another property owner's land. The earl and his hired men were definitely not considered good neighbors.

Griffith Evans was one of those who quickly sold some of his land to the earl. But many others of the early settlers were angry at the fraudulent land grab and spoke out against it. Among these were the Reverend Elkanah Lamb and Rocky Mountain Jim Nugent. Nugent trapped on the land and had a few cattle. Although Jim Nugent had once been a good friend of Griff Evans, the two men had a falling out over the earl and the land issue.

Another early settler who had no love for the Earl of Dunraven was Abner Sprague. Sprague and his partner, Clarence Chubbuck, found a good piece of land in what is today called Moraine Park, not far from Estes Park. They claimed it under the Homestead Act and began work on their homes. This piece of land had somehow been missed by the Earl of Dunraven during his gobbling up of land.

One morning, to the Spragues' astonishment, Theodore Whyte, the foreman for the Earl of Dunraven, came riding up and ordered them off this land. Sprague and his father stood firm. They insisted that the earl's claim to this piece of land was in error, and that it was legally theirs. On checking the facts, this turned out to be the case.

Soon after, Whyte and his men rounded up two hundred of the earl's cattle and drove them onto Sprague's land to graze in the Moraine Park Meadow. To be sure that the cattle stayed, Whyte put a salt lick there to keep the herd from straying. It was actions like these, completely disregarding legitimate claims and the rights of others, that made the earl so hated by many of the early homesteaders. No matter how much land the earl had, it was never enough.

When the earl's cattle were driven onto his land again, Abner Sprague saw what was happening and knew that it was but one of a number of tricks that the Earl of Dunraven and his agents employed to drive off legitimate homesteaders. Sprague, however, was not about to leave. After the earl's men had left, Sprague got his trusty herding dog, rounded up the two hundred head of cattle, and drove them right back to the earl's land in Estes Park. Not willing to give up, Whyte and his men again drove the herd back to Moraine Meadow. Again Sprague drove the herd off his land and back to Estes Park.

This time when Sprague drove the herd back and off his land, he made it a point to find Theodore Whyte. As Sprague later described it, "We had quite a wordy row." Whatever was said, it seemed to have been enough to make Whyte stop bothering Sprague, although on behalf of the earl, he continued to harass others.

The Earl of Dunraven could not have anticipated that more and more settlers would come pouring into the area by the mid-1870s. But they proved to be his undoing. Many of these people either ignored or disputed the earl's rights to the land that he had bought from men who really had never homesteaded or lived on the land. The Earl of Dunraven was finding out that maintaining his scheme was time consuming and costing him money. Perhaps it was time to make his property provide a return for his investment. The earl reluctantly had to reconsider his original plan to preserve this entire area as a vast hunting park for himself and his friends.

In 1876 the Colorado Territory became a state. The Rocky Mountain wilderness was no longer quite so wild. More and more people were coming to settle or simply to visit and vacation. Instead of resenting incursions to his private hunting land, the earl began to think of ways to capitalize upon all these newcomers to the Estes Park area and the growth and change that was taking place. He already had a cattle ranch. Why not add a big hotel?

The earl announced plans to build a hunting lodge at Dunraven Glade on the north fork of the Big Thompson. Theodore Whyte would serve as the manager. Griff Evans had done quite well with small cabins that he built around his own home to accommodate guests, and Mrs. Evans did the cooking for them. While this was satisfactory for a few visitors, the earl envisioned a grander plan. He would build a great facility and attract visitors from all over the world.

To help him pick the perfect site for a splendid new hotel, the Earl of Dunraven brought the famous German painter, Albert Bierstadt, to Estes Park in 1876. Not only was Bierstadt commissioned to paint a landscape of Estes Park and Longs Peak for which the earl paid $15,000 and later shipped home to his castle, but he was also asked to select the perfect site for the earl's hotel.

The site chosen for the new hotel was on the eastern side of Estes Park near Fish Creek. Although the official name of the hotel was the Estes Park Hotel, and although the Earl of Dunraven was a member of the Irish peerage, he apparently appeared English enough to the locals that everyone referred it to as the "English Hotel." It was a three-story, timber-frame building. A long porch ran the full length of the front of the building and halfway around each end. This new lodge opened in the summer of 1877. Near the hotel was a private cottage for the earl, who continued to make annual visits.

Others saw economic opportunities in the land at the same time the Earl of Dunraven was trying to corner the market. Among these early settlers were Alexander MacGregor who obtained land on the northern edge of the park in 1873 and Horace Ferguson who homesteaded near Mary's Lake. J. T. Cleve started a store at the junction of the Fall and Big Thompson Rivers in the early 1880s. And at the base of Longs Peak, the Reverend Elkanah Lamb homesteaded and developed a lodge for visitors that he called Longs Peak House. In addition to offering lodging, the Reverend sometimes guided hikers to the top of the peak.

Abner Sprague credits the many tourists in the area for saving even more land from falling entirely into the hands of the Earl of Dunraven. It was hard to make a living farming or raising cattle in this area, but when tourists started coming, a large number of the early homesteaders survived by taking in boarders. Otherwise, many of these early settlers in the area might have moved away and been forced to sell out cheaply to the earl. He or his agents were always about, eager to buy up any available pieces of land.

Some tourists came by stagecoach from Longmont, through Lyons, and into Estes Park. They traveled on a toll road that had been built by Alexander MacGregor's Estes Park Wagon Road Company. Some tourists came in two-horse wagons that had canvas covers that could be pulled back to allow visitors to see and enjoy the scenery. These were equipped with tents, blankets, food, stove and cooking utensils, and table furniture. Tourists enjoyed the out-of-doors in comfort and style. Campers might stop in at Sprague's or at the Reverend Lamb's for a hearty meal indoors. Many of these tourists brought with them fishing equipment or guns so that they could fish and hunt as well as follow trails and climb mountains.

During the 1870s, the Estes Park area also saw the arrival of a number of prospectors. No great strikes were made in the area, however. Then on July 10, 1875, two prospectors, Alexander Campbell and James H. Bourn, staked a claim in a mine they called the Wolverine. It looked promising and a rush of prospectors into the

Never Summer Range followed. The mine did not live up to its promise, and the owners sold out after a year.

Although none of the strikes near Estes Park proved rich, some small businesses did well in providing supplies to miners. It was not long before Estes Park became a village with a few shops and even a post office.

In 1878 the Larimer County Board of Commissioners found a way to benefit from the earl's land grab. They increased the assessments on the earl's cattle and put a tax on his sawmill. The earl found himself in constant litigation and objected to the exorbitant land taxes that he now faced. He became increasingly disenchanted with Estes Park. In fact, in a letter that he wrote to Lord Bernard Fitzpatric in October 1879 he said, "it wouldn't exactly break my heart if I was never to set eyes on Estes Park again."

There were a few small problems with his cattle ranching, too. A grand jury indicted Theodore Whyte and Griff Evans on nine counts of brand altering. Again, not content with the land and cattle they had purchased, they had added a little cattle rustling to their assets. There is no record of a verdict in the case, but just the fact that it was filed was no doubt another source of time-consuming irritation to the earl. At some point, he realized that his scheme for a gigantic hunting preserve had turned into a gigantic problem, and he didn't need it.

The earl did not return to Estes Park after the late 1880s. He served Queen Victoria as undersecretary of the colonies from 1885 to 1887 and commanded a battalion of sharpshooters in the Boer War. Disputes over claims and taxes caused the earl to completely abandon plans for Estes Park. In his own words, the earl wrote, "The show could not be managed from home, and we were in constant danger of being frozen out. So we sold for what we could get and cleared out, and I have never been there since." Even so, the earl revealed his fondness for the area when four years before his death in London in June 1926 at eighty-five, the earl wrote, "But I would love to see again the place I knew so well—in its primeval state."

In 1905 a small group of businessmen led by Cornelius Bond bought some of the land and organized the Estes Park Town Company. They divided the land into lots that quickly sold and the village began to grow, offering everything tourists might need. It was incorporated in 1917 and by that time boasted a hotel, a laundry, a stage station, and several general stores.

In 1908 B. D. Sanborn and F. O. Stanley succeeded in purchasing the remainder of the Earl of Dunraven's property, about six thousand acres. They set about turning the area into a premier resort. The famous English Hotel burned to the ground in 1911, although the earl's cottage survived. The gigantic land grab of the Earl of Dunraven, circumventing the intentions of the Homestead Act in favor of creating a private hunting preserve, failed. The earl's love of hunting and the outdoors made him greedy for this land. The strength of a few homesteaders willing to fight back and the growth of tourism in the area helped bring his jerky plans to an end.

SOURCES

Bancroft, Caroline. *Estes Park and Trail Ridge: Their Dramatic History*. Boulder, CO: Johnson Publishing Co., 1968.

———. *Trail Ridge Country*. Boulder, CO: Johnson Publishing Co., 1968.

Buchholtz, C. W. *Rocky Mountain National Park: A History*. Boulder, CO: Colorado Associated University Press, 1983.

Hicks, David. *The Estes Park Land Grab*. www.ghhs.us/Dunraven.htm.

———. *Lord Dunraven, The Earl of Estes*. Estes Park, CO: Estes Park Trail, 1968.

Jessen, Kenneth. *Colorado Gunsmoke: True Stories of Outlaws and Lawmen on the Colorado Frontier*. Boulder, CO: Pruett Publishing, 1986.

————. *Colorado's Strangest: A Legacy of Bizarre Events and Eccentric People.* Loveland, CO: J. V. Publications, 2005.

Pickering, James H. *This Blue Hollow.* Boulder, CO: University Press of Colorado, 1999.

Wyndham-Quin, Windham Thomas. *Canadian Nights: Being Sketches and Reminiscences of Life and Sport in the Rockies, the Prairies, and the Canadian Woods*, 1914.

Wyndham-Quin, Windham Thomas. *Past Times and Pastimes, Vol. II*. London: Hodder and Stoughton, 1921.

CHAPTER 4
Griffith Evans

THE MURDER OF ROCKY MOUNTAIN JIM

Many people have read the romantic tale of how Lady Isabella L. Bird in 1873 made her famous ascent of Colorado's Longs Peak assisted by Rocky Mountain Jim. Fewer people are familiar with Jim's murder. Rocky Mountain Jim (aka James Nugent) was gunned down by Griffith Evans on June 19, 1874. Although the reasons for the shooting are in dispute, there was no question about who did the shooting. In addition to the report of at least one eye-witness, Griff Evans himself readily admitted he had discharged both barrels of his shotgun.

Rocky Mountain Jim, mortally wounded, lived for several weeks, long enough to file charges before he died in September. His details of the shooting were published in the Fort Collins newspaper, the Standard. *Although Griff Evans was never punished for his crime, he'll forever be branded a jerk for shooting and killing his longtime rival, Rocky Mountain Jim.*

It was a peaceful scene, two men watering their horses in a small mountain stream. Suddenly the door of a nearby cabin was flung open and Griffith Evans stepped out holding a double-barreled shotgun. Without warning or provocation, he fired. A man beside him urged Evans to fire again. The first shot killed the horse and the second struck Jim Nugent in the head. Nugent did not die immediately, but he lasted only a few weeks. The first murder in Estes Park had just been committed.

The man who had been shot was James Nugent, known as Rocky Mountain Jim. Nugent was a fanciful character. Above all he was a great storyteller, especially about events of his early life. He spun stories about having been born in the South, being

Griffith Evans
COURTESY COLORADO HISTORICAL SOCIETY

a nephew of Civil War General P. G. T. Beauregard, and working as a trapper for the Hudson's Bay Company. He also talked about being a British Army officer, and at other times he claimed to be a former schoolmaster or a defrocked priest. He spun so many yarns that the truth of his youth is a mystery.

Nugent's adult life, once he arrived in Colorado, is much better documented. Shortly after his arrival he was camping at Grand Lake and went out walking with his dog. They came upon some deer, and Nugent's dog chased after them into the bushes. When the dog came running back out, it was followed by a cinnamon bear and her two cubs. Since he was near his camp, Jim had not bothered to bring his rifle with him, although he did carry a revolver and a knife.

The huge creature came at Nugent, and he fired his revolver into the bear five times. He finally stopped the bear but not before he was badly injured. He managed to mount his mule and head for Grand Lake. Several times along the way into town, he reported, he lost consciousness and fell off, only to remount and continue.

Men in Grand Lake helped Nugent as best they could and sent for a doctor. He had recovered enough by August to leave Grand Lake and eventually to build a small cabin in an area near Estes Park called Muggins Gulch. Nugent had lost an eye in his fight with the bear and one side of his face was terribly disfigured. Nugent lived alone and survived by keeping a few cattle, trapping, and hunting. He became part of the Estes Park settlement.

Only a few years earlier in the fall of 1859, this area got its first permanent white settler and its namesake, Joel Estes, who with his wife Patsy and their children came as part of the 1859 gold rush. Estes settled as a farmer in the valley. He and his family built a home and had the vast area largely to themselves. Estes soon found that the winters were very hard both on his family and on his herd of cattle. He gave up and moved away in April 1866.

The land on which Joel Estes had ranched passed quickly through a variety of hands. It went to John Hollenbeck for about nine months who then sold it to a Mr. Jacobs. Griffith Evans, a relative newcomer to Colorado, was hired to care for the ranch of Mr. Jacobs. Evans had moved to Colorado from Wisconsin where he had been a farmer. When they first arrived, Evans and his family lived for a short time in Golden City, Colorado. They welcomed the opportunity to move on to Estes Park. A friend drove Evans and his family with their very few possessions to the Jacobs' ranch in the fall of 1867 and the family moved into what had once been Joel Estes's log cabin. For provisions they had brought with them a little flour and potatoes; they hoped to live on whatever game Griff Evans could kill.

Although a variety of lone hunters and prospectors came through during the next few years, Evans was really the only permanent rancher in the valley until groups of settlers started arriving in 1874. In addition to tending the herd of Mr. Jacobs and grazing a few of his own cattle, Evans expanded his house and built extra cabins nearby where he would take in an occasional guest. Evans supported his family mainly by hunting. He would send his game by wagon to Denver and sell it in the open market. In addition, he continued to care for cattle. Gradually he built up a sizable herd of his own and took on partners and hired hands.

Eventually other homesteaders arrived including Rocky Mountain Jim Nugent, Abner Sprague, the Reverend Elkanah J. Lamb, Horace Ferguson, and Alexander MacGregor. Still, there were only a few people in the pristine area, and it remained quiet in this beautiful valley.

In those early years, Evans and Nugent both had some cattle and did a lot of hunting. They spent considerable time together. As time passed, however, their interests diverged. Instead of devoting his energies to ranching, Evans came to think that he could make a better living providing food and lodging for the many visitors that were now pouring into the area. Evans soon tore down the shanty lean-tos near his home and replaced them with fancier log cabins with stone fireplaces. He enlarged his own cabin, adding a big living room with a fireplace, couch, and lounging chairs for guests. He also dammed up Fish Creek and created a little pond where his guests could easily catch trout. He had founded the first resort in the area.

Griff Evans was gaining a reputation as a good host. In an 1873 letter to her sister, Lady Isabella Bird described Griffith Evans as "short and small, hospitable, careless, reckless, jolly, social, convivial, peppery, good-natured . . . He is a splendid shot, an expert and successful hunter, a bold mountaineer, a good rider, a capital cook, and a generally 'jolly fellow.'" Griff Evans's prized possession was a harmonium, or reed organ, and he delighted in playing music and singing for company.

Evans also knew the power of advertising. Since he had a virtual monopoly on the tourist trade in the area, he tried to make his hospitality known. There were not only articles in Longmont's *Colorado Press*, but he also had a short interview with a correspondent in the *Chicago Tribune*. In one of the Longmont articles, the correspondent wrote, "The reputation of Estes Park as a resort is world wide. Its cool and limpid waters, its splendid carriage drives, grand and awe inspiring scenery, luscious trout, and last, but not least, the genial smiling face of mine host, makes it a general favorite with all who have the good fortune to cast off the cares and worries of business, and seek shelter within its invigorating shade for a few weeks during the summer days."

It was only natural that when he came to the Estes Park area, the Earl of Dunraven, Windham Thomas Wyndham-Quin, would choose to stay with Griff Evans. The wealthy Earl of Dunraven was a passionate big game hunter, and he quickly fell in love with this spot of the world that was filled with deer, elk, bear, and sheep. The earl also brought with him a good liquor supply.

It was known that Griff Evans enjoyed drinking. In the early days of Estes Park, when he and Rocky Mountain Jim were very friendly, they often drank together. With the arrival of the Earl of Dunraven and his wealthy friends as paying lodgers, Griff Evans had new drinking buddies, and Rocky Mountain Jim was displaced.

Although he was wealthy, the Earl of Dunraven faced a problem in buying a substantial part of the area for his personal use.

Dunraven was prohibited from buying land available under the Homestead Act because he was not a citizen. He could circumvent the law, however, by buying land from United States citizens who had already claimed it. The earl quickly bought a piece of land from Griff Evans for $900. He was also able to buy property from others who had settled in the area.

Near the entrance to Estes Park, Rocky Mountain Jim owned his piece of land and cabin at Muggins Gulch. The Earl of Dunraven and his guests had to ride through Rocky Mountain Jim's land to get to the Dunraven place. At first, there was no problem. The earl and his guests had free access across the land. But before long, Rocky Mountain Jim took a dimmer and dimmer view of what he saw as the earl's land grab. Nugent finally took a real dislike to the earl and announced that he would not permit the earl and his friends to cross his land.

At this time only one road led into Estes Park. Riders had to come from Lyons, up the North St. Vrain River, north over Rowe Hill, past Granny May onto the Little Thompson River, and eventually follow the Little Thompson to Muggins Gulch. That was exactly where Rocky Mountain Jim lived. Because of the placement of his property, Jim Nugent became a real problem for the Earl of Dunraven, and he was not the least interested in solving it by selling his property to the earl.

The earl wasn't the only enemy that Rocky Mountain Jim made. One story suggests that Lord Dunraven began using the services of an Englishman named Hague in his various schemes to buy up additional land in Estes Park. Hague, in turn, hired Rocky Mountain Jim for $100 to ride to Denver and bring Hague's girlfriend up to Estes Park. When Jim Nugent returned from his mission a week later, he was alone. He reported that the woman did not want to come and spend her summer up there. Hague then accused Nugent of being a thief and a liar. Not one to take insults meekly, Nugent knocked Hague off his horse and forced him to retract what he had said.

Another rumor circulated that Nugent had been paying too much attention to Griff Evans's seventeen-year-old daughter,

Jennie. This was not acceptable to Evans. On top of all this, Evans and Rocky Mountain Jim increasingly were seeing one another as rivals in providing guiding services for tourists.

Evans sometimes guided visitors to the top of Longs Peak. In September 1873 Evans guided Anna Dickinson and Ralph Meeker from the ranch to Ferdinand Hayden's geological survey crew at the base of the peak and continued with them to the summit. Rocky Mountain Jim was also a guide up this mountain. That same year he had taken Lady Isabella Bird up and down Longs Peak. Griff Evans and Rocky Mountain Jim each disparaged the route that the other used to reach the peak.

Isabella Bird, in writing about her experiences with Rocky Mountain Jim, records, "He hates Evans with a bitter hatred, and Evans returns it, having undergone much provocation from Jim in his moods of lawlessness and violence, and being not a little envious of the fascination which his manners and conversation have for the strangers who come up here."

Whatever the reasons, a murder was about to take place. On June 19, when Rocky Mountain Jim and his friend, William Brown, stopped to water their horses on the way to Muggins Gulch, Griff Evans rushed out of his cabin and fired his shotgun. Hague was there with Evans and, according to most stories of the event, was egging him on to shoot. Apparently Evans and Hague had been drinking at the time of the shooting. Accounts agree that whatever the underlying motive, it was a cowardly surprise attack and Jim Nugent did not draw a weapon.

In his book *Early Estes Park*, Enos Mills writes that Brown, who was with Rocky Mountain Jim at the time of the shooting, gave Mills this firsthand account: "Evans took the gun and as Jim passed near, fired two shots in rapid succession, and without warning." Another resident of the area, Abner Sprague, wrote a very similar account based on what Brown, the eyewitness, had told him of the incident.

Surprisingly enough, Jim Nugent did not die immediately. He was carried back to his own cabin and tended by Dr. George

Kingsley. At the time of the shooting, Dr. Kingsley was out hunting a bear. Three riders came and got him to come and see Jim Nugent. The doctor found that most of the gunshot had gone right through the body, but one piece had lodged in the brain. Rocky Mountain Jim was taken to Fort Collins, and two more doctors were called in. Nugent lived for several weeks before dying on September 7, 1874.

Living as long as he did after the shooting gave Jim Nugent time to blame his death on Griff Evans. In an article that appeared in the Fort Collins *Standard* newspaper on August 12, Nugent wrote, "On the 10th day of June 1874, while riding peacefully along a highway in company with one William Brown, when near the residence of one Griffith Evans, he approached me with a double barreled shotgun in his hands, and when within a few steps, without warning, raised his gun and fired, killing the horse I was riding and inflicting a wound upon my person which fell me to the earth, and after I had fallen he deliberately walked up and shot me again through the head, turned upon his heel and disappeared in his house without even the inquirey [sic] whether I was dead."

Jim Nugent filed charges, and a warrant was sworn out for the arrest of Griff Evans. Hague (Haigh) was also named as an accomplice in the shooting because he was present and shouted out encouragement for Evans to shoot Nugent again. The court met in Fort Collins, and the prosecuting attorney did not bother to come and hear Nugent's side of the story even though he was less than a mile away. Instead the attorney not only filed a charge against Griffith Evans for assault and battery with intent to kill, but in a surprise move, also convinced the jury to indict Jim Nugent for assault with the intent to kill Hague. This charge was made solely on the evidence of Evans and Hague who maintained that Evans had shot Nugent only because he feared Nugent had come by the cabin to kill Hague.

Some newspaper reports at the time also indicated that Evans had shot Nugent at the instigation of the Earl of Dunraven. Evans was released to hunt up $2,500 in bail, while Hague went free without bail. And it was announced that when Jim Nugent was well enough to be moved, he would be escorted by the sheriff to jail.

The filing of charges eventually led to some interesting results. Hague was tried as an accomplice because after the first shot, he cried out, "Give him the other barrel." Hague testified that Rocky Mountain Jim had threatened him several times with a gun. The judge apparently believed him and therefore thought that Hague was justified in making the comment.

Amazingly, Griffith Evans was also found not guilty. The judge maintained there was lack of evidence since William Brown, the man who was with Jim Nugent at the time of the attack, had disappeared before the trial took place. Local rumor had it that the Earl of Dunraven had paid Brown to vanish. Of course, the only other person present at the shooting was Jim Nugent, and by the time of the trial he had died. In July 1875, it was decided there would be no other prosecution of the case against Griffith Evans.

Griff Evans finally left Estes Park in 1878, turning over his holdings to the Earl of Dunraven's foreman, Theodore Whyte. He moved to Lyons and then Jamestown. Evans allowed the local church to use his beloved harmonium, and as he grew old became a "resident father Christmas" because of his long, white beard. After all those years, no one cared or remembered that Griff Evans was the jerk who had murdered Rocky Mountain Jim.

SOURCES

Bancroft, Caroline. *Estes Park and Trail Ridge: Their Dramatic History.* Boulder, CO: Johnson Publishing Co., 1968.

———. *Trail Ridge Country.* Boulder, CO: Johnson Publishing Co., 1968. An especially good source for names of historic figures and places in Colorado history.

Bird, Isabella. *A Lady's Life in the Rocky Mountains.* London: Virago, 1982. Based largely on notes and letters to Lady Isabella Bird's sister.

Buchholtz, C. W. *Rocky Mountain National Park: A History.* Boulder, CO: Colorado Associated University Press, 1983. A detailed book on all aspects of the park.

Dunning, Harold M. *The Life of Rocky Mountain Jim (James Nugent).* Boulder, CO: Johnson Publishing Co., 1967.

Jessen, Kenneth. *Bizarre Colorado: A Legacy of Unusual Events and People.* Loveland, CO: J. V. Publications, 1994.

———. *Colorado Gunsmoke: True Stories of Outlaws and Lawmen on the Colorado Frontier.* Boulder, CO: Pruett Publishing, 1986.

Mills, Enos. *Early Estes Park.* Denver, CO: Hirschfeld Press, 1972.

Pickering, James H. *This Blue Hollow.* Boulder, CO: University Press of Colorado, 1999.

CHAPTER 5

Alferd Packer

CANNIBAL AND LIAR

*W*hen accounts of rich gold strikes in the San Juan Mountains
*of Colorado began to circulate throughout the country in
1874, another small gold rush began. Alferd Packer joined a group
of men from Utah heading to Colorado to try their luck at prospecting. Twenty-one men set out in his group. They had high hopes but
low provisions. Worst of all, they started out during snowy weather.
They ignored the advice from Chief Ouray—whom they met along
the way—to wait a few more weeks. Impatient, and angry with each
other, they split into three small groups to journey onward. After
considerable hardship, the members of the first group arrived at
the Indian Agency.*

*Weeks later Alferd Packer, who was in the second small group
to leave Chief Ouray's camp, arrived at the agency alone. None
of the others in his group made it. Packer gave many differing
accounts of what had happened during the journey. What each of
these accounts had in common was a confession of theft, murder,
and cannibalism. Whichever version of the fate of the small group
of men was true, and however much hardship and suffering those
men faced, one fact remained: Alferd Packer was a liar and a jerk.*

In April 1874 a lone prospector, Alferd Packer, came walking into
the Los Pinos Indian Agency in Colorado. He had a Winchester
rifle over his shoulder, his feet were wrapped in strips of blanket,
and his hair was matted. The employees of the Indian Agency who
saw him approaching rushed to bring him inside. When he was
asked about the five other men who had been with him, Packer
stated that he didn't know where they were. He explained that
the original large group had broken into three smaller groups. In

Alferd Packer
COURTESY COLORADO HISTORICAL SOCIETY

fact members of the first group that had left ahead of Packer had arrived many days earlier at the agency. Packer explained that while traveling with his small group, he injured his leg, fell behind, and became separated from the others. In fact, he expressed surprise that the others hadn't arrived well ahead of him. Packer insisted he didn't know where they might be.

Days passed and the other members of his party never appeared. Men from the first group of the original Utah party also noticed that Packer now had money. They knew that when he started the trip in Utah, he was poor. Where had the money come from? Suspicions were aroused. It was suggested that Packer lead a search party back up the trail he had come to find the missing men. He did so, but the search was unsuccessful when Packer became confused and said he couldn't locate the exact route he had traveled.

Then came disturbing reports that up the trail from which Packer had so recently emerged, mutilated bodies had been found in the snow at what seemed to have been a prospectors' camp. During questioning, Packer kept changing his original story of what had happened on the journey. An investigation began. Could Packer be both a murderer and a cannibal?

His birth certificate gives his name as Alfred Packer, but he sported a tattoo that spelled his name as Alferd Packer. He is known to have used both names. Packer was born on November 21, 1842 in Allegheny County, Pennsylvania. Before leaving home and striking out on his own, Packer apprenticed in a small printing establishment. Holding a job and searching for employment was made difficult because he sometimes suffered from epileptic seizures. These seizures were at times severe. His desire to cover up this affliction was no doubt one of the reasons why Packer lied so glibly and so frequently.

On April 22, 1862, during the Civil War, twenty-year-old Packer joined the Sixteenth Infantry in Winona, Minnesota. He was honorably discharged from the Union army on December 29, 1862, as "incapable of performing the duties of a soldier because of Epilepsy." Packer didn't give up serving in the army easily. He tried to cover up his disability and joined the Iowa cavalry. Again he was discharged. After that, Packer held a number of different jobs including teamster, miner, hunter, trapper, and guide. While working in Georgetown, Colorado, as a miner, he lost portions of the index and little fingers of his left hand. These physical deformities combined with a high, raspy voice made him easy to identify and remember.

Packer left Colorado and moved to Utah where he lived in the town of Sandy, twelve miles south of Salt Lake City. He worked in a smelter and did a little mining without much success. News reached him of rich ores being discovered in the San Juan Mountains of Colorado. Learning of a small group of men being organized to go to Colorado, Packer decided to join them. The group had horses and wagons and were taking travelers with them for a fifty dollar fare. The fifty dollars would pay for a man's transportation and provisions. Packer had very little money, but he agreed to pay twenty-five dollars and work out the rest by tending two four-horse teams on the journey.

The group of men who headed for Colorado ranged in age from the eldest, Israel Swan, who was almost sixty, to the youngest, George Noon, who was only nineteen. Among the party were several prospectors, a butcher, a physician from Scotland, a Frenchman named Jean "Frenchy" Cabazon, two Irishmen, and a young man known as Italian Tom.

In late autumn 1873, the party of men left Bingham and picked up Preston Nutter and his wagon and team in Provo, Utah. In Salina they picked up the last member of their group, a man who had journeyed there by stagecoach. Now numbering twenty-one men, they started on their 325-mile journey to the Colorado border. They followed the Mormon Trail that had been used earlier by Brigham Young and also by the Pony Express. They hadn't gone far before they discovered that their supplies were low and game was scarce. They survived for a time on chopped barley, which had been brought along as food for the horses.

The crossing of the Green River, eighty-five miles from the Colorado border, was especially difficult. They ended up making a raft. They disassembled the wagons, ferried them over, and re-assembled them on the other side of the river. This proved very time consuming. They started traveling again only to find themselves surrounded by Native Americans who took them to the camp of Chief Ouray about two miles south of present-day Delta. Ouray welcomed them, and the weary men rested for a while in camp. In time they grew restless, and in spite of the winter cold eleven of the men elected to leave and continue their journey.

Chief Ouray told these men to follow the Gunnison River to "cow camp," a government cattle camp, "seven suns" away. There they could get provisions before following the creek to the Los Pinos Agency, after which it was forty more miles to Saguache. Before they left Ouray's camp, however, there was a dispute among the eleven men and they broke into two groups. Five men left on February 6, became lost, and nearly starved. But after three weeks, they managed to reach the government cattle camp. They rested and went on again in spite of further terrible travel conditions. They were half-dead when they finally succeeded in reaching the Los Pinos Indian Agency.

Alferd Packer and his group of six left Ouray's camp on February 9, 1874. They had provisions for about ten days. Two of the men had rifles, one a skinning knife, and one a hatchet. Packer was unarmed. Thinking the trip would take about a week, they hiked off in a southeasterly direction and almost immediately found themselves in the midst of a snowstorm. It was sixty-five days later, on April 16, when Packer, all alone, arrived at the cow camp and was taken in. Packer told the story that he had been left behind due to fatigue, frozen feet, and snow blindness, and said he had continued on his own.

Packer repeated this story not only to strangers but also to those at the agency who had been in the original large party from Utah. Preston Nutter was one of the original party who had seen the other two small groups leave but had decided to remain in

Chief Ouray's camp until the weather improved. He had only recently arrived at the Los Pinos Agency after an uneventful two-week journey.

Packer eventually went on to Saguache with two of the men from the original prospecting party. He spent quite a bit of time in the Saguache saloon, repeating his story. Still the other five men from his small group never appeared. The missing men and the fact that Packer suddenly seemed to have quite a bit of money made his earlier companions suspicious. One member of his old traveling party noticed that Packer now carried a knife that had belonged to one of the other prospectors in Packer's party.

When Packer bought a horse, a saddle, and clothes, he paid one hundred dollars in cash, and the seller observed that Packer took some of the money from each of two billfolds. The Indian agent, Charles Adams, and his wife stopped in Saguache on their way back to the Los Pinos Reservation from Denver. When Adams heard all the stories about the missing prospectors and all the money Packer was spending, he also grew suspicious.

Adams suggested that Packer come back with him to the agency to lead a search party for the missing men, which Packer agreed to do. Adams asked Packer where he got the funds he was spending, and Packer told him the money was a loan from the village blacksmith. When Adams checked on Packer's claim, he learned it was a lie. No loan had been made. Thoroughly alarmed now, Agent Adams began a long interrogation of Packer.

Packer eventually gave a confession that was quite different from the story he had told on arrival. He said that winter weather had quickly overtaken his little party of prospectors, and they were near death from cold and starvation. Sixty-five-year-old Israel Swan died about ten days into the trip. Packer stated he was eaten by the five survivors. Four or five days later, James Humphrey was eaten. Then Frank Miller died from an accident and he, too, was eaten. With only three men left alive, Packer said that Shannon Bell killed nineteen-year-old George Noon and then came after Packer with a hatchet. Packer said he shot Bell in self-defense.

Adams wrote down this version of the events, woke up the justice of the peace, and had Packer sign his confession in the presence of the justice of the peace. The Indian agent also sent a report of this version of Packer's confession in a letter to his superior, the Commissioner of Indian Affairs in Washington, D.C.

The search party for the bodies, which Agent Adams organized, failed when Packer said he was lost at the point in the trail where the searchers approached the Lake Fork of the Gunnison River. The members of the search party were suspicious enough of Packer that they wondered if he might have killed the others in his group and dumped their bodies in the lake. The searchers actually broke up a beaver dam to lower the water level and carry out a water search. They found no bodies.

After the search party returned to the agency, Packer was arrested on suspicion of homicide even though no bodies had been found. Since there were no jails available at the agency, Packer was sent to Saguache where a small stone structure on Sheriff Amos Wall's ranch was used as a jail.

Of course the case drew attention and filled the local papers. It wasn't long before a reporter appeared on the scene from *Harper's Weekly* magazine. A huge story broke when the bodies of the missing men were finally found. There are at least two reports about how the bodies of the prospectors were discovered. One version states that around August 20, an artist who was in the area of Lake San Cristobal working on assignment for *Harper's* found the remains of five human beings. Another report, printed in the *Rocky Mountain News* on August 28, 1874, said that Captain C. H. Graham of Del Norte found the bodies.

Whoever found them, the bodies were relatively well-preserved in the snow, and they showed clear signs of mutilation. One was missing its head, which it was surmised might have been carried off by wild animals. The other heads showed signs that they had suffered blows, and all personal property was missing from the area except for a few blankets and tin cups. It did not look as if the men in the group had been camped long at the site, perhaps only for one night. There was no evidence of a struggle at the campsite. The area of the grisly find was promptly named "Dead Man's Gulch."

A coroner's jury was impaneled and an inquest was held at the scene of the murders. The remains were identified by one of the original twenty-one men who had set out from Utah. The bodies were buried on a high bluff nearby, and each grave was marked with a wooden post showing the name of the occupant.

Immediately a warrant was sworn out charging Alferd Packer with five counts of murder. The warrant was issued on August 22, 1874 in San Juan City, Hinsdale County. The handwritten warrant read, "Now therefore it is your duty to use all due diligence in arresting and bringing to Justice that said Al. Packer, and if taken, you are commanded to bring him before me . . ." Squeezed in after the phrase, "and if taken," was added "dead or alive." Before the warrant could be served, however, another piece of news broke. Alferd Packer had escaped from the irons at his makeshift jail on Sheriff Wall's ranch near Saguache.

The day of the escape, Sheriff Amos Wall was in district court at Del Norte. There were rumors that he may have been in collusion with Packer on the escape, but nothing was ever proved. Little more was mentioned about the murders or about Alferd Packer until a year later when a human skull was found about a mile from the murder site. There was speculation that this was the skull of Miller whose headless body had been found with the other murdered prospectors, and that animals had carried it off from the campsite. Interest peaked, and then faded.

Years passed before the name of Packer claimed headlines again, this time as the result of a chance meeting at Fort Fetterman. The fort was built to be used as a supply base in 1867 at the junction of La Prele and the North Platte River. It was located about 135 miles north of Cheyenne, Wyoming. Eventually the government gave up the fort and it was used by civilians. In one of the buildings travelers could obtain board and lodging. A frequent traveler who knew the fort well was "Frenchy" Cabazon, who had been with the original party of twenty-one prospectors who left Utah with Alferd Packer. Cabazon was now an itinerant peddler who sold household goods from his wagon.

In March 1883 Cabazon was in Fort Fetterman when he was approached by a man whose voice seemed somewhat familiar. The man gave his name as John Schwartze. Noting the missing fingers on the man's hand, Cabazon felt certain it was Alferd Packer. Cabazon, however, did not indicate that he recognized Packer and promised to pick up some mining tools that were requested and bring them back in his wagon on his next trip. Cabazon then reported to the deputy sheriff in the vicinity that he had found Alferd Packer.

A flurry of activity followed before Alferd Packer was arrested by Sheriff Malcolm Campbell of Converse County on March 14, 1883, about thirty miles from Fort Fetterman in Wagonhound where Packer had been living. Packer admitted that he had escaped from jail and had been passed a key to unlock the irons he was in, but he never identified who had helped him.

Packer was delivered to the sheriff of Hinsdale County in Cheyenne, placed in manacles, and escorted to Denver by train. When he arrived at Union Depot on March 16, about a thousand people turned out to catch a glimpse of him. By this time, the newspapers were calling him the "ghoul of the San Juans."

Back in the hands of authorities, Packer made a confession. This second confession was quite different from both his original story and the first written confession he had made. Now Packer claimed that his little expedition had run out of food on the fourth day but managed to survive for several more days on what little they could find, which was mostly rose hips and pine gum. Packer said that he went out to search for food, and when he returned to camp he found Shannon Bell eating Frank Miller's leg. The three others in the party had all been killed by a hatchet and were laid out next to the campfire.

When Bell then attempted to kill Packer with a hatchet, Packer said he shot Bell with his hunting rifle. When Bell fell forward and dropped the hatchet, Packer took up the hatchet and struck Bell in the head. This took place on about the eleventh day of the expedition. Since the snow was so deep that he could not travel, Packer said he remained there near the camp for sixty days, awaiting spring and surviving by eating his dead companions.

After making this second confession, Packer was escorted from Denver to Gunnison by train on March 18. Since Hinsdale County did not have funds for special guards, Packer was confined to a steel cell in the Gunnison County Jail. Although Packer had no money at this point, three lawyers agreed to represent him apparently because of the publicity they would get and the interesting aspects of the case. To make him more presentable, they promptly got their client a haircut and a new suit of clothes.

Newspapers not only released Packer's latest account of the death of his companions but accused him of all sorts of other crimes in Utah, Wyoming, and along the Continental Divide. He was described as "villainous," "ugly," and a "poisonous reptile." Although no trial had been held, most newspaper articles already called for his death by hanging.

A grand jury presented five indictments against Packer. There was considerable legal wrangling on how to proceed because the crime may have taken place on Native American land, or at least in Colorado Territory, well before Colorado achieved statehood. Who had jurisdiction? The original indictment was amended, with changes in wording about the place of the crime, and with a request for prosecution for only the Swan homicide rather than for killing all five members of the prospecting party. There was also a request to delay the trial because the residents of Hinsdale County had all been inflamed by the publicity. This last motion was denied.

On Monday, April 9, 1883, Alferd Packer's trial began in Lake City. The second story of the courthouse was filled with curious observers while witnesses, attorneys, and lawmen filled the first floor. Prospective jurors were questioned under oath. Many were rejected because they knew they were going to be called as witnesses in the case or because they admitted that they had already formed an opinion of Packer's guilt. Only five jurors were seated that morning. Late that afternoon, a jury of twelve was finally seated.

The trial began and witnesses were called. During the prosecution, testimony came out that Packer was in possession of Miller's skinning knife and that he had plenty of spending money. There was testimony about the camp and the condition and identification of the bodies. The confession that Packer had first made and signed was introduced in evidence. One witness, Otto Mears, testified that he saw a Wells Fargo draft in Packer's pocketbook and that Packer paid for goods purchased from Mears using cash that he took from two billfolds.

During the defense, Packer took the stand and testified for six hours on his own behalf. He said he wanted to tell what had happened without interruption and then would agree to be questioned. He also asked that certain men who had testified against him be in court to be called upon since he had no other witnesses. Although this was somewhat unusual, the judge and attorneys agreed.

Packer then described how his party ran out of food, and how one by one, the men had given up goat skin moccasins, which they roasted and ate. Packer testified that he left camp in search of food and returned to find the others dead and Bell ready to attack him with a hatchet. Packer said he killed Bell in self-defense by shooting him "sideways through the belly." (The prosecution later refuted this by stating that an examination showed Bell had been shot in the back. In 1989 Professor James Starr headed up a team that performed an exhumation at the burial site seeking forensic evidence. They reported in the *Loveland Reporter-Herald* in August 1989 that they found no evidence that any of the men had been shot.)

Packer testified that he didn't know how long he remained in camp after the killings. He admitted to taking money from the pockets of the dead men, and he admitted that the first story that he told when reaching the Indian Agency was not true and that he had lied again in the first confession that he made under interrogation.

After both sides had presented their case, the jury received its instructions and left at seven o'clock in the evening to deliberate. The next morning at nine o'clock, the jury was ready with its verdict. Packer was found guilty of the premeditated murder of Israel Swan. The members of the jury were polled, and they all confirmed the verdict. The judge then sentenced Packer to be hanged on May 19 in Hinsdale County.

The judge gave a long and rather eloquent conclusion before passing sentence on Packer. But when news of the judgment left the courtroom, someone (perhaps the Saguache bartender who had witnessed the trial) falsely quoted the judge as saying to Packer, "They wuz sivin Dimmycrats in Hinsdale County, and yer ate foive of them. . . . I sintins ye t' be hanged by th' neck until yez are dead, dead, dead, as a warnin' ag'in reducin' th' Dimmycrat populashion iv th' state."

Judge M. B. Gerry actually spoke in much fancier prose. On sentencing, he said, "Whether your murderous hand was guided by the misty light of the moon, or the flickering blaze of the campfire, you only can tell. No eye saw the bloody deed performed; no ear save your own caught the groans of your dying victims."

The defense attorney immediately submitted thirteen reasons why Packer's sentence should be reversed and why Packer should get a new trial. The Supreme Court agreed to consider the case, so the execution of Packer was stayed. Fearing a possible lynch mob, Packer was moved from Hinsdale County back to the secure Gunnison County jail.

It was not until December that Packer's appeal finally came before the Supreme Court. The Court reversed the original sentence on the basis of changes in the homicide statute that had been made in 1881. The Court called for a new trial on the charge of manslaughter. Packer's attorneys asked that the trial be moved from Lake City to Gunnison and this request was granted.

The second trial was set to begin in Gunnison on July 19, 1886. Before that date, Packer's attorneys appealed and asked that Packer be set free because the statute of limitations had run out on the new charge of manslaughter. This appeal was denied, and the judge then ordered that all indictments for the deaths of the five men be considered for trial before one jury.

On August 2, the second trial began and again it was difficult to impanel a jury. Evidence was presented as before, and Packer again chose to take the stand in his own defense. The jury came back with a finding of guilty of manslaughter.

The judge asked Packer if he had anything to say before sentence was passed. Packer made a rambling statement saying that he had only killed one man and that eventually the whole matter would be cleared up. The judge then sentenced Packer to forty years, eight years each for the killing of five men. So thirteen years after the event, Alferd Packer was finally convicted of his crimes.

In Canon City, Packer conducted himself as a model prisoner who had many visitors, tended a garden plot, and made handcrafts that he sold or gave away. Several times he filed a petition for pardon without success. In 1893 a Denver attorney took his case and argued that there was no precedent for having five indictments heard in one trial before one jury. The Colorado Attorney General answered that Packer had consented to this and had not immediately entered an appeal and that now it was too late. Next, a commission was created to decide if due to his epilepsy or "insanity," Packer should be released. It was the commission's decision that Packer remain in jail.

While Packer's 1899 appeal for pardon was still pending, Mrs. Leonel Ross O'Bryan, known as "Polly Pry," entered the picture. She was associated with the *Denver Post* and was a colorful and powerful figure in American journalism for over three decades. Once she took an interest in the Alferd Packer case, she wrote many articles on his behalf. At that time, Charles S. Thomas was governor of Colorado, and he denied Packer's latest request for a pardon in a statement published in the *Denver Times*.

On January 3, Polly Pry wrote a long article in the *Denver Post* attacking the governor's decision to keep Packer in prison, stating that Packer was convicted "on the flimsiest sort of circumstantial evidence." She also suggested that the governor was unduly influenced by Otto Mears, with whom the governor had discussed the case and the appeal.

Along with her article, Polly Pry printed the names of those who had signed a petition she had circulated on Packer's behalf. It included the names of judges, key officials in Denver's leading banks, the superintendent of Denver's schools, the U.S. district attorney, numerous sheriffs, officials of the Union Pacific, Denver's mayor, and Thomas M. Patterson, a rival politician who hoped to be appointed by the legislature to be the next senator from Colorado. It was well known that Governor Thomas had his eye on serving in that same senate position as soon as he completed his current term as governor.

The sensational newspaper article was followed by more rebuttals and articles, for and against Packer. Then a bizarre turn of events occurred. A meeting was held in the offices of the *Denver Post* with editors Bonfils and Tammen and Polly Pry present. They met with William W. Anderson, a well-known Denver attorney. Earlier, Anderson had gone to visit Packer and secured a complete power of attorney. Believing this was not in Packer's best interests, Polly Pry got Packer to revoke the power of attorney. An angry meeting took place in the editor's office. According to one account, Bonfils at one point leaped to his feet and struck the attorney beneath his eye. Bonfils and Tammen threw Anderson out of their office. Anderson jerked the door back open, pulled out his gun, and fired four shots, wounding both editors. Anderson was arrested and charged with assault.

When Anderson was tried for assaulting the editors, Packer was called in to testify about his earlier meeting and granting the power of attorney. Packer conducted himself well in court, and reporters began to write of him as a "misjudged and persecuted man." The jury could not come to an agreement in the Anderson case, and so he was found not guilty.

Then quite suddenly and without warning on January 7, 1901, outgoing Governor Charles S. Thomas, in his last act as governor of Colorado, granted Packer parole due to his "physical condition and advanced age." He had served fifteen years of his sentence. Packer left the penitentiary and went straight to Denver to thank his old friend Duane Hatch and Polly Pry for working so hard to release him. During that first week of freedom in Denver, the state legislature chose the new U.S. senator from Colorado. Rather than choosing former governor Thomas, they selected Thomas M. Patterson, who had signed Packer's release petition.

Packer saw the sights of Denver before moving to live in Sheridan, Colorado, where he tended a garden and kept rabbits and chickens. He spent much of his time in Deer Creek Canyon, about twenty miles from Sheridan. There he prospected among abandoned mining claims.

In 1906 Packer suffered an epileptic fit while in Deer Creek Canyon. He was found by a game warden who brought him to the home of Mrs. Van Alstine. He refused hospitalization and lingered on being tended in the home for several months. On April 17, 1907, Packer wrote to Colorado governor Henry A. Buchiel asking for an unconditional pardon. No action had been taken on this last request before Alferd Packer died on April 24, 1907.

No matter which of the versions of the deaths of the prospectors is correct—whether there was cannibalism and/or multiple homicides—Alferd Packer admitted to killing a man and lying about it, and in so doing he behaved like a jerk.

SOURCES

Fenwick, Robert W. *Alfred Packer: The True Story of Colorado's Man-Eater.* Denver, CO: *Empire Magazine* of the *Denver Post,* 1963.

Jessen, Kenneth. *Colorado's Strangest: A Legacy of Bizarre Events and Eccentric People.* Loveland, CO: J. V. Publications, 2005. A collection of very short, unusual stories.

Kushner, Ervan F. *Alferd G. Packer, Cannibal! Victim?* Frederick, CO: Platte 'N Press, 1980. The author of this book, a former judge, admits that he disagrees with the belief expressed by many others that Packer was guilty of five murders. He has circulated a petition for a posthumous pardon. The book gives attention to the legal aspects of the case and actual testimony.

CHAPTER 6

Doc Holliday
and Bat Masterson

THE COLORADO RAILROAD WAR

*T*he *Denver and Rio Grande Railroad and the Atchison, Topeka
and Santa Fe Railroad were at war. The 1872 rush of prospectors into the Arkansas Valley yielded an abundance of new mines.
Each of the two railroads was determined to be the one to lay the
tracks and carry the ore for this new bonanza. It was a no-holds-
barred fight for control. Every dirty trick imaginable was played to
slow up the other railroad. Under cover of darkness, pieces of finished track were mysteriously destroyed. Tools disappeared. Bullets occasionally whizzed by, driving workers away from their tasks
to take cover.*

*Two famous gunmen, Doc Holliday and Bat Masterson, were
hired to enter the Colorado Railroad War, and in playing their
roles, they sometimes found ways to behave like jerks.*

People called it the Roundhouse Battle at Pueblo, and what a fascinating battle it was, surely the most memorable of the Colorado
Railroad War. Bat Masterson had been hired by the Santa Fe to
defend the railroad, and he was in command of about fifty handpicked gunmen, including Doc Holliday. Through the influence
of wealthy Santa Fe Railroad officials, Masterson had just been
appointed a United States deputy marshal. By this ploy, the Santa
Fe Railroad could pretend that they were doing nothing more than
legally defending their property.

Battle lines were drawn. On one side was Masterson and his
hired guns. On the other side was Deputy Sheriff Pat Desmond
along with the sheriff and officials of the Rio Grande and their

DR. JOHN H. HOLLIDAY
The gun-fighting dentist who was known as the coldest-blooded
killer of the West. This photograph, made by C. S. Fly in Tombstone, 1881, was the only one 'Doc' Holliday ever had taken.

©History Colorado

John Henry "Doc" Holliday
COURTESY COLORADO HISTORICAL SOCIETY

armed men, prepared to charge with fixed bayonets. Was this going to be a last stand of some sort? Were the railroad guards and the gunmen actually going to engage in a shoot-out at a railroad roundhouse? How had two famous gunmen gotten themselves into the middle of a railroad war?

Silver miners in the late 1870s rushed into Colorado's upper Arkansas Valley in search of rich ore in what was known as the Leadville District. Where there is an abundance of mining, railroads are needed to carry the ore to refineries. The Denver and Rio Grande Railroad and the Atchison, Topeka and Santa Fe Railroad already had tracks in the Arkansas Valley. The Rio Grande had a line near Canon City; the Santa Fe had a line in Pueblo.

West of Canon City, the Arkansas River cuts through rock, forming a steep, narrow gorge through which water rushes. Both the Rio Grande and the Santa Fe Railroad wanted to build track through this narrow canyon. On April 19, 1878, a Santa Fe Railroad construction crew began grading to lay track at the mouth of the gorge. Only a few hours later, the Rio Grande rushed their construction crews to the same spot. They already had existing track less than a mile from Canon City. When the Rio Grande crew arrived, their way was effectively blocked by the Santa Fe graders. This marked the beginning of what would turn out to be a two-year battle that came to be known as the Colorado Railroad War.

The two railroads persisted in laying track and in doing everything possible—legal and otherwise—to disrupt the work of the other. An unusual number of "accidents" occurred. Rocks mysteriously dislodged and came tumbling down onto newly laid track. Work crews were shot at by riflemen. At night essential tools would mysteriously move from their resting places and end up in the river. Both railroad crews built stone forts overlooking the gorge at strategic points, such as Fort DeRimer built by the Rio Grande crews at Texas Creek.

As part of their daily equipment, railroad crews now carried or had at hand not only picks and shovels, but pistols and rifles as well. Both sides soon felt it was necessary to hire armed guards.

William Strong of the Santa Fe contingent went with five hundred riflemen to make sure that Raton Pass stayed in their hands. The Santa Fe sent a representative to Dodge City in March 1878 to recruit mercenaries. Both Doc Holliday and Bat Masterson signed up along with other gun fighters to ride in wagons into the Royal Gorge to protect the survey and work crews.

The gathering together of these armed guards by the railroad companies made for some strange combinations. Deputy Sheriff Pat Desmond of Pueblo had worked with and assisted Deputy Sheriff W. B. Bat Masterson of Ford County, Kansas, in arresting a cattle rustler and escapee from the Dodge City jail. Now the two men found themselves on opposite sides during the railroad war.

Newspapers began weighing in. The *Rocky Mountain News* favored the Denver and Rio Grande, but the *Denver Tribune* sided with the Santa Fe. While tempers were flaring and men were shooting, it was of course inevitable that numerous actions of the railroad war would end up in court. A court decision in early 1879 gave both railroads the right to use the Royal Gorge.

The Atchison, Topeka and Santa Fe Railroad asked for an injunction to stop the Denver and Rio Grande Railroad from trying to build their track. On June 10, the Fourth Judicial Circuit ruled in favor of the Rio Grande. This court decision meant that the lawmen of the various counties involved had to help enforce the court decision.

Bat Masterson and Doc Holliday were at the roundhouse at Pueblo. It had been chosen as a defense line. Bat Masterson, as a U.S. marshal working for the Santa Fe, was charged with keeping control of a facility that the courts had now decided was not operating legally. Masterson's men were not only armed with rifles, revolvers, and shotguns, but they had also secretly acquired a Gatling gun, a sort of old-fashioned machine gun.

Deputy Sheriff Pat Desmond, along with the sheriff and officials from the Rio Grande Railroad, met to discuss ways in which they could drive Bat Masterson and the other gunmen from the roundhouse at Pueblo. One suggestion that came out of this

William Barclay "Bat" Masterson
COURTESY COLORADO HISTORICAL SOCIETY

meeting was to take the Gatling gun that was stored in the state armory. When they tried to put that plan into action, they found out to their chagrin that Bat Masterson had already taken it. They realized he might use it against them.

Nevertheless Deputy Sheriff Pat Desmond prepared to fight using the weapons that he had. He gathered fifty Denver and Rio Grande railroad guards with plenty of ammunition and rifles with fixed bayonets attached and prepared to attack. They charged on the station platform and telegraph office, forcing the men inside to run out the back doors and windows. One man was shot. Desmond and his men zeroed in on the next target: the roundhouse. Realizing they faced expert marksmen and a machine gun, reinforcements were brought in. A Rio Grande train brought in General William J. Palmer, head of the Denver and Rio Grande, along with several hundred armed men to surround the roundhouse.

At this point, under a flag of truce, one of the treasurers for the Rio Grande came out carrying a small black satchel and met with Bat Masterson. No one knows of course exactly what was said during the meeting that lasted for about an hour. The result was clear though. Bat Masterson and his gunmen surrendered the roundhouse without a shot. Reports suggest that Masterson accepted and divided up among his men a ten-thousand-dollar bribe.

Bat Masterson went back to Dodge City to serve again as Ford County Sheriff while Doc Holliday returned to gambling in Trinidad. Holliday didn't stay there long before he was involved in a shooting and moved on to Las Vegas, New Mexico.

An appeal to the United States Supreme Court resulted in the Denver and Rio Grande Railroad being granted the primary right to build in the Royal Gorge, where there was only room for one track.

Having lost out in court, the Santa Fe Railroad—which was larger and wealthier than the Rio Grande—decided on another means of attack. They threatened to build track parallel to the Rio Grande and to compete with existing Rio Grande lines. Fearing that this would result in a great financial loss, the bondholders pressured the management of the Rio Grande to lease the existing railroad to the Santa Fe for a thirty-year period. The Santa Fe then manipulated freight rates from Kansas City making it more advantageous to use Santa Fe rather than Rio Grande lines, causing a substantial financial loss to the Rio Grande. This brought the matter back to a local court, which restrained the Santa Fe from operating the Rio Grande lines. The Denver and Rio Grande railroad men retook their railroad using armed force. Trains were taken over by armed men, depots and engine houses were fired upon, and a few men were killed.

The railroad war was not really resolved until March 27, 1880 when both railroads settled on what came to be called the Treaty of Boston. The Rio Grande paid the Santa Fe $1.8 million dollars for its work in the gorge so far, and the Rio Grande continued the construction work, with the railroad reaching Leadville on July 20, 1880.

•   •   •

How did two famous gunmen, Doc Holliday and Bat Masterson, who had made their reputations long before the Colorado Railroad War, become woven into history? John Henry "Doc" Holliday was born in 1852 in Griffin, Georgia, and graduated from Baltimore Dental School in 1872. He opened his first dental offices in Atlanta.

Shortly after he began his practice of dentistry, Holliday was diagnosed with tuberculosis. For his health's sake, he was encouraged to find a drier climate. In 1873 Holliday moved to Dallas, Texas, and opened a dentist's office there. At this time he began to gamble heavily and soon found gambling more lucrative than his dentistry. He also drank a good deal, saying he needed to drink because of his constant cough.

Holliday was known for his hot temper, and he found himself in trouble for trading gunfire with a saloonkeeper, although neither of the two men was injured. On May 12, 1874, Holliday was indicted in Dallas for illegal gambling. He moved to Denison, Texas, and then decided to leave the state altogether.

He continued his dentistry, but for the most part spent his time gambling as he visited the mining towns of Denver, Cheyenne, and Deadwood. When he returned to Texas in 1877, Holliday met Wyatt Earp. The two became friends. A year later in Dodge City, some cowboys who had lost money gambling seemed intent on killing Earp. Holliday defended Earp in a saloon battle, thus cementing their friendship.

Holliday often seemed to be involved in gunfights, although many of the tales about him were wildly exaggerated. Records indicate that throughout his life, he was arrested at least seventeen times, although only twice for murder. He was seldom convicted of anything. A newspaper reporter once asked him if his conscience ever bothered him, to which Holliday is credited with replying, "I coughed that out with my lung, long ago."

Both Holliday and Earp moved to Tombstone, Arizona, in 1880. They were involved in the famous gunfight at the OK Corral in October of 1881. An inquest held after the shoot-out determined that neither Earp nor Holliday had "committed a criminal act." That did not satisfy those whose friends and relatives had been killed. In the weeks that followed, Earp's two brothers were ambushed and killed. Fearing more trouble, Earp and Holliday went to Tucson. There they were involved in the death of Frank Stillwell, who supposedly was still hunting down Wyatt Earp because of the OK Corral. Although there was no proof as to exactly who had shot Stillwell, this is the crime that much later came to haunt Holliday.

When Doc Holliday moved to Pueblo, Colorado, he decided it would be wise to start out with a new name; he called himself Tom McKey. He didn't stay long in Pueblo but moved on to Denver where he became a faro dealer at a local gambling spot called Babbitt's House. He worked an eight-hour shift, and when he wasn't working, he often went gambling himself. One of his favorite spots was Big Ed Chase's place. Sometimes he took short trips into mining camps such as Black Hawk and Central City. He also left for a time to go to Cheyenne, Wyoming, but he always returned to the faro table at Babbitt's.

At that time Denver had a law against carrying firearms. Many of the local citizens ignored this law, but Doc Holliday, still known as Tom McKey, obeyed it. Instead of a gun, he carried a knife. Tom McKey built up his reputation when one night an angry customer, not knowing that he was facing the notorious gunman, Doc Holliday, pulled out a gun at his faro table. Holliday didn't hesitate—he leaped at the man, overpowered him, and wounded him with his knife. This taught the gambling community to fear Tom McKey.

In addition to gambling, Doc Holliday proved himself a jerk by running a very successful con game using the Union Pacific Railroad. He would board a train and pretend to be a mine owner or engineer, carrying with him a phony gold brick in a bag. Doc would find a sucker, secretly show him the gold brick, and tell him some wild story about how it had been stolen and came into his hands. Holliday would offer to sell it cheap. Once the victim of the con had paid for the worthless brick, Doc Holliday, using the name of Tom McKey, would leave the train. Suddenly two men, posing as detectives from Pinkertons, a private security guard and detective agency that often worked for railways, would appear, demand the gold brick, and threaten the victim with arrest. The result was that the victim would pay a substantial bribe to keep the Pinkerton men quiet and would hand over the "stolen gold brick." At this point, although he'd paid twice for a worthless brick, the victim was happy not to have been thrown in jail and wouldn't raise a fuss. Tom McKey would meet up with his buddies, reclaim the brick, and be ready to try the con again.

For a time Holliday—still using the name of Tom McKey—moved to Trinidad where he worked as a peace officer while also gambling. This was fairly common. The thinking was that if any violence broke out in one of the gambling places, a law officer would be on hand to deal with it. On May 10, 1882, Doc Holliday went back to Pueblo, this time using his own name. One day, a man came up to him, thanking Doc for having saved his life in Santa Fe, and showed him what he said were bullet wounds. This stranger also warned Doc that someone was coming in on the train and would attempt to shoot Doc.

Holliday dismissed the matter. He didn't recognize the man or any of the events he talked about, and he didn't think the so-called bullet wounds were real. But when Holliday attended a horse race in Denver on May 14, the stranger, who now gave his name as Perry M. Mallen, stopped Doc again. This time Mallen had with him two sheriff's deputies with guns drawn.

Mallen identified himself as a deputy sheriff and said he had been hunting Doc for seven years for a killing that took place in Utah. He went on to accuse Doc of numerous charges including the murder of a railroad conductor, a cattle rancher, and others. Holliday denied the charges but was taken to jail. He sent for Bat Masterson. Holliday and Masterson were not close friends, but both were good friends of Wyatt Earp, and they had their Colorado Railroad War connection as well.

Masterson quickly traveled to Denver. He realized that Mallen was a fraud and that the murder charges in Utah were false, but he also knew that if the sheriff who now had Doc Holliday in custody extradited him to Arizona, Holliday might well be convicted there for helping Earp kill Frank Stillwell in Tucson. Local newspapers began weighing in, some championing Doc's cause and others demanding justice. The sheriff wired Arizona's governor asking for advice.

To avoid having Doc extradited, Masterson made up a crime. As a U.S. marshal he charged Holliday with having taken one hundred fifty dollars in a confidence game. A warrant was issued for Doc's arrest on this bunco charge. The judge discharged Holliday, preventing him from being extradited to Arizona, Doc was arrested on the fake charge, and Masterson moved him immediately to Pueblo. Doc appeared before a Pueblo judge on the charge of swindling, and paid bail. Other charges could have been pursued in district court, but Holliday left, and no trial took place.

After that Holliday spent his final years in Colorado. He lived in Leadville and later on in Glenwood Springs where he went for the waters. He died on November 9, 1887, at the age of thirty-six.

•   •   •

William Barclay "Bat" Masterson seems to have led two lives. The first was as a gunman and a lawman in the wild West, which sometimes brought him into Colorado. The second was as a fight promoter and sports writer in New York.

William Barclay Masterson was born between 1853 and 1855. Accounts differ as to whether he was born in Quebec or in the United States. He grew up on farms in Canada and the United States until 1870 when his family homesteaded in Wichita, Kansas. From there, Masterson and his older brother moved west and were employed as buffalo hunters and hide skinners. At this time Masterson met Wyatt Earp, who would remain a friend for life.

Around 1874 Masterson visited Dodge City, Kansas, and then moved on to Sweetwater, Texas. In a saloon in Sweetwater in a fight over a girl, Masterson killed a man in a shoot-out and was injured. After that he became famous for carrying a cane, which he sometimes used in fights. By 1877 he was back in Dodge City, where he served as deputy undersheriff to Wyatt Earp. Masterson was then elected sheriff of Ford County. He was made a deputy U.S. marshal in 1879 just before taking on his stint for the Atchison, Topeka and Santa Fe Railroad during the Colorado Railroad War.

Masterson gambled and served as a lawman throughout the West in towns such as Leadville, Tombstone, and Trinidad. He married in 1891, and spent the next several years as a peace officer and as owner of a gambling house.

Masterson next moved to New York and found he enjoyed the city, especially its boxing venues. He became well known in town; the character Sky Masterson from *Guys and Dolls* was based on

Bat. Masterson met President Teddy Roosevelt, also a boxing fan, and the two became friends. Roosevelt often invited his friend to the White House and appointed Masterson as deputy U.S. marshal for the southern district of New York.

An old friend from Kansas, who was now managing editor of the *New York Morning Telegraph*, hired Masterson as a sports writer. Masterson wrote mainly about boxing, and quickly moved to be a regular columnist, and then became sports editor. He worked at the newspaper until his death on October 5, 1921.

Although Masterson and Holliday were not really friends and had interesting and varying careers, their involvement in the railroad wars, hiring out as mercenaries, avoiding a real fight, and accepting a bribe qualified them as jerks.

SOURCES

Churchill, E. Richard. *Doc Holliday, Bat Masterson, and Wyatt Earp.* Leadville, CO: Timberline Books, 1974.

Marshall, James. *Santa Fe: The Railroad that Built an Empire.* New York: Random House, 1945.

Myers, John. *Doc Holliday.* Boston: Little, Brown, & Co., 1955.

O'Connor, Richard. *Bat Masterson.* Garden City, NY: Doubleday & Co., 1957.

CHAPTER 7

John Gillis Mills, Sheriff Charles Royer, and Undersheriff William Redman

MURDER AT GRAND LAKE

*W*hat could have been more idyllic and all-American in 1882 than celebrating the Fourth of July in the great outdoors at Grand Lake, Colorado?

Two county commissioners and the county clerk had just enjoyed a good breakfast at the Fairview House and were hiking down to a meeting at the Grand County courthouse when shots rang out. It was neither fireworks nor firecrackers. These were gunshots. Two men fell. More shots rang out. Two more men were hit.

Masked gunmen made a quick getaway. When the truth became known, it was not some notorious gang members who had done the shooting, but a small group of local men led by John Gillis Mills, the Grand County commissioner, supported by none other than Sheriff Charles Royer and his undersheriff, William Redman. The actions of these two lawmen on this day revealed them to be jerks.

It was a hot Fourth of July and the three men who had just enjoyed a hearty breakfast at the Fairview House in Grand Lake, Colorado, walked down toward town where they were scheduled to hold a meeting. Fireworks of one kind or another had been popping off all day.

When shots rang out, those who heard them thought it was part of the ongoing celebration. But the three men knew better when one of them was struck by a bullet and fell to the ground. The others tried to help their friend and got off some shots themselves

William Redman
COURTESY COLORADO HISTORICAL SOCIETY

before the attackers fled the scene on horseback. Four men lay dead or dying on the ground.

The location of a county seat of government could be a very important issue during the early days of Colorado history. Disputes over such matters were common, but it was not common to argue the matter to the point of murder.

At one point in time, Grand Lake was a very quiet settlement. There were a few friendly Native Americans, some fishermen, hunters, and trappers. Most of the few visitors who came stayed in the Wescotts' cabins. When miners started pouring into the area, Grand Lake quickly changed. The Grand Central Hotel was erected on Grand Avenue. In 1881 another hotel, Garrison House, went up at the west end of the lake, facing Mt. Craig.

That same year, Fairview House went up. It was two stories high and L-shaped, and was built by the old pioneering custom known as "house raising." In isolated communities, neighbors came and pitched in to build a house or barn, and in addition to hard work, the event was a social activity, too. The hostess in this case, Mrs. Mary. J. Young, provided a hearty noon meal for all of the men who had come to work on her building. After sundown, she also served a big dinner. That night, as was often the custom, there was a fiddler and a dance. Fairview House took its place in the growing town of Grand Lake.

Up to this time, Hot Sulphur Springs had been the county seat, but with the 1879 mining boom that saw more and more settlements going up around Grand Lake, people began to question whether the county seat should be moved. The argument over the location of the county seat for Grand County became a bitter one, but no one could have guessed that it would lead to a number of deaths.

To many it seemed that Hot Sulphur Springs, located on the road over Berthoud Pass, was the logical choice. It was the center of ranching in the county. Others favored Grand Lake, pointing out that the population there had grown from thirty-one people in 1880 to three hundred by 1883. There was an economic shift, and the mines of Grand Lake now seemed more important than ranching. Grand Lake citizens believed that Hot Sulphur Springs was too far west and too remote from the growing population of the North Fork mines to be the county seat.

Eighty-one citizens of Grand Lake petitioned the county commissioners to hold an election to determine the county seat. When the election was held on November 2, 1880, Grand Lake won the popular votes for county seat by a count of 114 to 83. The board of commissioners at that time, however, was predominantly made up of men from Hot Sulphur Springs. Rather than accept the vote, they disallowed enough of the ballots to adjust the outcome in favor of Hot Sulphur Springs, and ruled that the county seat would not be moved. According to Colorado law, another vote on determining a county seat could not be held for four years.

Obviously tempers were high. On April 9, 1881, recently seated board members took action. One commissioner, John Gillis Mills, had been a Chicago lawyer. When capital from Cook County, Illinois, was invested in mines near Gaskill and Teller, Mills moved to Teller City where he practiced law. He was an influential and savvy man, and he soon became chairman of the board of county commissioners. He favored Grand Lake for the county seat.

Another Chicago lawyer in the area was Edward P. Weber. He had been sent out by Chicago investors to watch over their interests and he soon became manager of the Wolverine Mine. Weber favored Hot Sulphur Springs for the county seat. In the early days, these two men appeared friendly, but each was ambitious.

When the Republican county convention was held in the autumn of 1882, both Mills and Weber were candidates to be delegates to the state convention in Denver. It was clear that each wanted to control Grand County. Both realized that to be successful and to move up in politics, they needed supporters.

Mills made friends with Charles Caswell, a North Park rancher. Weber became friendly with Thomas J. "Cap" Dean, who lived in Hot Sulphur Springs, and with Barney Day, also a county commissioner. Day owned a ranch between Hot Sulphur Springs and Kremmling. Through lots of political maneuvering, Mills and

Caswell were selected as the official delegates from Grand County to go to the Denver convention. Weber and Dean went to the convention anyway as a rival delegation from Grand County. They somehow convinced the Republicans to seat them as the official delegates. This started a personal feud between the two former Chicago lawyers. Mills was also angry at Weber over their disagreement about the location of the county seat.

Battle lines were drawn and both men continued to build a power base. Mills won over to his side Charles W. Royer, the sheriff, and William Redman, the undersheriff of Grand County. Sheriff Royer was described as a friendly and amiable character. Almost everyone seemed to like and admire him. But he was often dominated by his powerful undersheriff. William Redman was active and aggressive. He was over six feet tall and noted for his powerful build, remarkably large feet and hands, and frequent involvement in quarrels.

It was easy for Redman to fall in with Mills, because he already had a grudge against Weber. He blamed Weber for scaring off some investors who had been interested in buying Redman's mining property. Redman reportedly threatened Weber's life over the loss of the $4,000 he had hoped to receive in the land sale. Redman had also quarreled with Dean over a cattle sale. In fact, in 1877 Redman was arrested for attacking Dean and knocking him down. The case was eventually dismissed by a county judge and never came to trial.

Mills supported Grand Lake for county seat, and he insisted that the election canvassers had exceeded their legal rights in declaring many of the ballots void. He stated they had falsified the election returns to keep the county seat in Hot Sulphur Springs, and that Grand Lake was the legal county seat. At his insistence all the county offices were therefore moved to Grand Lake. Builders were hired to construct a $350 courthouse and a jail in just forty-eight hours.

That did not end the dispute. Those on the side of Hot Sulphur Springs, including Weber, were determined to win back its place as county seat. Powerful men worked to achieve this. One was

William N. Byers, the former editor of the *Rocky Mountain News.* Another was Cap Dean. Dean took the matter to district court using the services of Weber as attorney. With Byers providing the financing, the matter went all the way to the Colorado Supreme Court. In April 1882, a year after the election, the matter was sent back to the district court and they found in favor of Grand Lake.

Mills used his power as county commissioner to make road improvements that favored the mining interests of the Grand Lake area. Funds were not well managed or accounted for, and by the end of 1882, Grand County had a debt of $12,000. Mills kept making new allies and aligned himself with a wealthy Georgetown mine owner.

Weber and Dean openly criticized the work of Commissioner Mills. The local Grand Lake newspaper, the *Grand Lake Prospector*, stood behind Mills and called Weber and Dean "small-brained" and "cowardly." When one of the county commissioners retired, the governor appointed Weber to the board. This put the two enemies, Mills and Weber, on the same board. Although they now had to work together, they still did not speak to one another. Weber began to be the dominating force on the board.

July 4 fell on a Wednesday in 1882, and the county commissioners were to meet that week on Tuesday. The district court was in session, and Mills was on the docket to appear in a divorce case. He requested that the county commissioners meet instead on Thursday, July 5, so that he could participate, and his request was granted.

Weber and Day, however, went ahead and held a secret county commissioners meeting on July 3, appointing a temporary clerk for the meeting. They voted to raise the bonds of the county officers who were not on their side of the county seat dispute to the sums of $20,000 and $30,000. They hoped this would oust Mills and his friends who would be unable to meet the bond. Then Weber and Day would rescind the vote about bonds and appoint their own supporters.

Although the July 3 meeting was secret, somehow Mills learned that it had taken place and what had transpired. Commissioner

Mills plotted an attack against his enemies for the Fourth of July. Whether he actually intended to kill them or simply frighten them is uncertain. One report notes that he said he wanted to have fun and "scare hell out of Weber and Day." Some reports state that Mills carried with him a forty-foot length of rope, and that he had said unless Weber agreed to rescind the bonding order, he was going to threaten Weber with hanging.

In Mills's small band was Charles Royer, sheriff of Grand County, William Redman, undersheriff, and Redman's brother, Mann, who always seemed ready for any sort of excitement. All the men carried revolvers, and Mills also carried a carbine. The men wore handkerchief masks. They tethered their horses nearby in some bushes and took up positions behind conveniently located rocks.

It was after eight-thirty in the morning on July 4 when county commissioners Barney Day and Edward P. Weber, accompanied by County Clerk Thomas J. "Cap" Dean, began walking down a wagon road from the Fairview House toward town. They strolled along the west shore of Grand Lake. Weber was unarmed. Day carried a .45 caliber revolver, and Dean always carried a Colt Navy model revolver.

There are two firsthand accounts of what happened, and the accounts are very similar. One account comes from Dean, who was wounded in the shoot-out and finally died of his wounds on July 17.

According to Dean, a rifle shot rang out and Weber cried out that he had been shot. Day and Dean reached out to catch him and assist him to the ground. At this point the masked men who had been waiting in the nearby clump of trees and rocks jumped out. One of the men carried a smoking carbine. The ambushers began shooting at Dean and Day. Day was the next one hit, but he pulled out his own revolver and started firing back. He shot and killed one of the men wearing cloth masks and he wounded another before he himself was shot dead. At this point the attackers ran for their horses and escaped.

At first no one was aware that there had been an attack. Since it was the Fourth of July, the gunshots seemed to bystanders to be no more than firecrackers. A mortally wounded Weber with a bullet through his lungs slowly tried to make his way back to the Fairview House while bleeding profusely. People finally realized what had happened and rushed to help. At the scene, Day was found dead at the lakeshore, and Dean was badly wounded, unresponsive, and lying face down.

One of the masked gunmen had also been shot dead. When his mask was removed he was proved to be John G. Mills. The wounded men were brought back to the Fairview Hotel. A doctor was summoned for Weber, but he died without regaining consciousness. Only badly wounded Dean could try to tell what happened. It was time to start an investigation. But where were Sheriff Royer and his Undersheriff William Redman? Only later did people begin to wonder when Dean's description of one of the attackers sounded suspiciously like William Redman. Because the assailants were wearing masks, Dean said he could not be absolutely certain, nor did he know exactly how many men were in the group of attackers.

Those at the scene learned that Day's revolver had been fired four times, Dean's revolver had not been fired, and Mill's rifle had been fired once. They also saw a trail of blood leading away from the lake for a quarter of a mile.

Sheriff Royer turned up later that day in Hot Sulphur Springs. His horse was reported to be lathered up as if it had been on a long, hard ride. He said he had been chasing one of the murderers. He then rode to Grand Lake, expecting that he would find no living witnesses, and was surprised to learn that Dean was still alive. Where was Redman? No one knew.

A message was sent to the nearest telegraph office to Colorado Governor James R. Grant. He considered sending out the militia to restore order, but because no clear reports were available, the militia was not sent.

Dean lasted a few days and then died of infection. He and Day were buried at Hot Sulphur Springs, while Mills was buried at Grand Lake Cemetery and Weber was buried at his ranch.

Only seventeen days later, there were shocking headlines in the *Colorado Miner*, the Georgetown newspaper. The headlines read, "More Blood: Charley Royer Blows His Brains Out in Georgetown."

Sheriff Royer had taken a room in Georgetown at the Ennis house; his body was found there in a pool of blood. He had his revolver at his side. An inquest was held with the verdict that Royer had committed suicide. At first it was believed that the pressure from the shoot-out and the suspicions thrown on his undersheriff were simply too much for Sheriff Royer and he shot himself. No one wanted to believe that the sheriff was in any way involved in the murders at Grand Lake.

One of the sheriff's friends, Adam Kinney, kept secret for several years the fact that Sheriff Royer had told him before going to Georgetown that he could no longer live with murders on his conscience. Kinney stated that the sheriff confessed to him in detail what really happened at the shoot-out and how the sheriff had participated in the killings. He reported that Mills had shot and killed Weber and that Redman had wounded Dean. Then Mills ran out and began beating Dean with his gun. To protect his friend, Day shot and killed Mills. Day then ran near an ice house at the lake and fired at and wounded Redman. To protect his undersheriff, Sheriff Royer killed Day.

Royer's suicide brought the death total of the Grand Lake shoot-out to five. It remained uncertain whether others were involved in the incident and what happened to William Redman. Undersheriff Alonzo Coffin and J. Gilman Martin were suspected of being in on the plot. On August 20, 1883, in district court, these two men and William Redman, who did not appear in court, were charged with murder.

Coffin and Martin pled not guilty and were released on bond. The testimony against them by a local surveyor was suspect, and by the time the case came to trial, two witnesses had disappeared.

One story says that a body believed to be Redman was found near the Ouray Indian Agency in southwestern Colorado on August 7. This find was reported and investigated by Major J. F. Minniss. A short distance away from the body, a saddle was found with "William Redman" scratched on it. Since there was cash on the body and the Colt revolver had been fired once, Major Minniss believed this was a suicide.

Another story alleges that Redman was hidden by his wife until he recovered, and that he then shot a man, scratched his name into the man's saddle, and left it where it would be found and lead people to think he had killed himself. And yet another account claims that Redman was never apprehended but that he committed suicide near Encampment, Wyoming. Others maintain that he was never found.

At least one Grand County resident, Bob Wheeler, says that Redman escaped to Arizona. Wheeler says he saw Redman years after the shooting in a small town in Wyoming.

After all the bitterness and murders, what happened to the county seat? The mining boom ended in Grand Lake, and by 1886 almost all the mining on the North Fork stopped. Small mining camps were abandoned. Grand Lake increasingly turned to the tourist trade rather than mining for its support. Because of these factors, including a declining population, the county seat was moved from Grand Lake back to Hot Sulphur Springs in 1888. This time, no jerks appeared with guns to contest it.

SOURCES

Bancroft, Caroline. *Trail Ridge Country.* Boulder, CO: Johnson Publishing Co., 1968.

Buchholtz, C. W. *Rocky Mountain National Park: A History.* Boulder, CO: Colorado Associated University Press, 1983.

Jessen, Kenneth. *Colorado Gunsmoke: True Stories of Outlaws and Lawmen on the Colorado Frontier.* Boulder, CO: Pruett Publishing, 1986.

CHAPTER 8

Silver King Horace A. W. Tabor

THIRTY-DAY SENATOR AND WIFE-DITCHER

*O*nce you've earned the name of "Silver King," a senate seat *is surely not too high to aim, and why not a beautiful new queen to go along with it? Although he provided generous support to Republican campaign funds, causes, and candidates in hopes of one day being rewarded with a choice political office for himself, H. A. W. Tabor indulged in too many indiscretions to hope for election to the U.S. Senate. His longtime wife Augusta had created quite a scene when he decided to ditch her in favor of the company of a beautiful young divorcée. With this notoriety, Tabor's cronies could not give him a long-term senate seat, but in recognition of his generous donations of a million dollars or so, they could provide him with a thirty-day term, long enough to satisfy his ambitions. Thirty days as an interim senator was enough for Tabor to enjoy the Washington scene and to hold a magnificent wedding reception for his new bride—and to prove himself an unparalleled jerk.*

The Washington wedding in the spring of 1882 appeared to be a perfect storybook affair. The gorgeous blonde bride in her twenties, decked in white satin and carrying white roses, wore a string of pearls purported to have belonged to Queen Isabella of Spain. The groom, though more than twice the age of the bride, was a handsome United States senator. The guests included the president of the United States. The ceremony, which began at nine o'clock, was officiated by Rev. P. L. Chapelle, priest of St. Matthew's Catholic Church. The reception that followed was lavish with its wedding cake and flowers.

But all was not quite as it seemed. Certainly the priest was not aware that the bride had been divorced and that she had already

H. A. W. Tabor
COURTESY COLORADO HISTORICAL SOCIETY

secretly married Tabor before coming to Washington, D.C. Perhaps he was the only one at the ceremony who did not know—or at least pretended not to know—about Tabor's first wife, Augusta, who had only recently been discarded.

It took a rather remarkable string of events for this wedding to occur. An assassin had shot President James A. Garfield, and Chester A. Arthur succeeded him. President Arthur named Senator Henry M. Teller of Colorado to be his secretary of the Interior, and Colorado Governor Pitkin appointed George M. Chilcott to temporarily fill the senate vacancy until the legislature met to elect Teller's successor. When the legislature met, they would select a new senator for a six-year term, and they would also elect someone to serve the remaining thirty days of Teller's unexpired term.

The Colorado Republicans faced a dilemma. They could not afford to offend Tabor because of his generous funding of Republican campaigns and causes, but they dared not make him a six-year senator due to all the unpleasant recent publicity about him divorcing his wife and carrying on a public affair with another woman. He also had made enemies by interfering in the miners' strike in Leadville. The solution? See if Tabor would be agreeable to a thirty-day term and would continue to donate large sums of money to support the party. It was agreed. Tabor was appointed U.S. senator from Colorado on January 27, 1883. He would serve as senator until the beginning of the new six-year term, which would go to Thomas M. Bowen as of March 4, 1883.

Tabor was happy for even the short term in the Senate. It is rumored that he sent a case of champagne to every member of the state legislature who had elected him. He also sent whiskey and wines to his friends at the Leadville *Herald*. The newspaper was promptly filled with news of his election and pictures of the Silver King. The very next day, Tabor was off to Washington in a private and very expensive train. His new love, Baby Doe, had to wait patiently in Denver.

Once in Washington, Tabor rented a suite of ten rooms on the second floor of the Willard Hotel located at Fourteenth Street and

Pennsylvania Avenue. In his luggage Tabor had packed a new nightshirt made of silk and lace with gold buttons, which had cost him $1,000.

Tabor quickly took in the Washington scene with visits to theaters, restaurants, and bars as well as attending busy meetings with colleagues on the floor and in the cloakrooms of the Senate. He brought dozens of influential men home for drinks. He found the time to offer a bill to protect Colorado forests and one to establish a military post in western Colorado. He served on a standing committee on pension and claims. The record shows that he was also absent from the Senate for sixteen days of his thirty-day appointment.

Why was he absent? Tabor's interest was not in serving in the Senate. He was there to make plans for a very special and elaborate wedding. Baby Doe arrived in Washington on March 1. Tabor presented her with a diamond necklace for which he paid $90,000. Since Baby Doe insisted on being married by a Catholic priest, Tabor found one, giving him a big enough fee so that the priest did not inquire about the fact that both Tabor and Baby Doe were divorced.

Important guests were invited, including President Arthur, Secretary of the Interior Teller, distinguished diplomats, and the entire Colorado congressional delegation. Most of the wives of these statesmen, however, refused to attend. Their sympathies were with the discarded Augusta. Still his generous gifts of champagne to various newspaper offices back in Colorado assured that there was plenty of coverage of his wedding in the society pages. Baby Doe brought her father, two brothers, and two sisters from Wisconsin to attend the ceremony.

The day of the wedding, Tabor had a special gift for his bride. He had delivered to her a string of pearls. They had been sold to him by men purporting that they had once belonged to Queen Isabella of Spain. The men had supposedly gone to Portugal and Spain to make the purchase, although they had actually bought the pearls in New York.

• • •

Who was this Senator H. A. W. Tabor and how did he reach this point? Horace Austin Warner Tabor was born in Vermont on November 26, 1830. Tabor's mother and father had been born in New England. He lived and went to school in the small farming village of Holland where his father was a tenant farmer. Tabor worked for a time in a general store. When his mother died and his father remarried, Tabor left the farm and was apprenticed to a stonecutter. He followed this career at several quarries for about eight years.

In August 1854, Tabor, now twenty-two, went to work for a well-to-do Maine contractor. After a couple of years, he asked the boss's daughter, Augusta, to marry him. They were married after a two-year engagement. The newly married couple homesteaded a 160-acre farm in Riley County, Kansas.

Farming life was hard and not very profitable. Both Horace and Augusta did what they could to earn money. He worked at Fort Riley, and she made a few dollars selling butter and eggs to immigrants who came through. The winter of 1858–59 was especially bitter, and the Tabor cabin was almost buried in snow.

When news of the Colorado gold rush came, Tabor decided to head west. He gave Augusta the choice of coming with him into the goldfields or returning to Maine. She chose to set off with him for the Colorado goldfields. They left in an ox-drawn covered wagon on April 5, 1859, along with their young son, Maxey, and two good friends, Samuel B. Kellogg and Nathaniel Maxey (after whom Tabor's son was named). They started out on their trip well supplied with blankets, a cook stove, potatoes, corn, coffee, and smoked meat.

For a time the journey was smooth. Then they crossed what is now the Kansas-Colorado border and grass became scanty. The oxen were weak. The travelers had no more meat. Facing near starvation, they pushed on and arrived in Denver on June 20. They had been on the trail for two and a half months. On her arrival, Augusta Tabor became only the eleventh woman in town.

At this point in time, the Colorado Territory was not yet organized. The whole area was part of the Western Kansas Territory.

After resting for two weeks in Denver, the little party moved first to Clear Creek, near the present town of Golden, and then to a mining camp, south of Black Hawk, in the Gregory Gulch region near what is now Central City, Colorado.

Augusta and Maxey stayed behind in a tent home while Tabor and his friends went out prospecting. They did not strike it rich, so they loaded up the wagon again and moved to the area now known as Idaho Springs. There they built a log house with a tent roof for Augusta and the baby.

While Tabor went out prospecting, Augusta started her own little business. She sold milk from the cows they had brought with them and also sold homemade meals, bread, and pies. She had learned to be self-sufficient. Again Tabor didn't make any rich strikes, but Augusta's business thrived and made them enough money to get them through the winter. The group moved once again, traveling through Ute Pass to South Park. They continued on until they reached a mining camp named California Gulch on May 8, 1860.

This time Augusta Tabor was the first woman in the mining camp. The men built her an eighteen-by-thirty-two-foot log cabin with a sod roof, and she quickly set up business again while Tabor went prospecting. Augusta took in boarders, did washing, and because they had gold scales, she also weighed gold dust. This camp was named Oro City after the Spanish word for gold. The little city began to live up to its name with many gold strikes, and before long the town was booming. Augusta Tabor was named postmistress of Oro City. She had the reputation of being an honest, hardworking woman.

By September of 1860, Tabor had accumulated five hundred dollars worth of gold dust. This meant that the family could leave the mountains that winter and go to visit with Augusta's father and mother. The money also allowed them to buy another tract of land, adjacent to the original one, in Kansas. The Tabors purchased a large amount of flour in Iowa on their way back to Colorado. This would be profitable in the store both for sale and for use in baked goods.

After returning to Oro City, Horace Tabor went prospecting again while Augusta opened her store. To earn extra money, she even rode on horseback to Denver to transport gold for the express office. During the summer of 1861, Augusta Tabor made more money from her store than her husband did prospecting for gold.

Once the easy-to-find placer gold gave out, the mining camps became deserted. So the Tabors moved again, this time to the other side of the Mosquito Range to a camp named Buckskin Joe. Again Augusta opened a store, which also served the camp as the post office. Tabor did poorly in his mining in South Park, and they lived off of the business. Tabor continued to dream of a big gold strike. He would often grubstake prospectors, giving them supplies in return for an equal share of any gold they might strike. Unfortunately, none of these prospectors had any better luck than Tabor.

In 1868 the Tabors returned to Oro City. They built a log cabin about a mile from the current site of Leadville. Again they opened and ran a general store. In addition, Tabor became the postmaster and express agent. At this time about 250 people lived in the town, which served as a county seat in the Territory of Colorado. In 1877, there was a second rush to California Gulch, but this time people were seeking silver rather than gold. The Tabors moved their Oro City store about a mile closer to town. Business now boomed enough so that the Tabors had to hire clerks to help out in the post office and their general store. They also opened a sort of bank since many people started depositing their funds in the Tabor safe.

At a town meeting held in January 1878, the people chose a new name for their town, Leadville, and voted H. A. W. Tabor to be their mayor. Although he was now a businessman, and a minor political figure, Tabor never gave up the idea of striking it rich in the mines.

Certainly rich silver strikes were being made, and many new prospectors were arriving. By January of 1879, there were over five thousand residents in Leadville. On April 21, 1878, two prospectors asked Tabor to grubstake them. They picked out what they needed, about seventeen dollars worth of supplies from the store, and signed an agreement saying that Tabor was entitled to one-third of anything they found. The prospectors chose a spot, registered a claim, and sank a shaft. Because one of the miners was from Pittsburg, they named their mine the Little Pittsburg.

Within a few days, the two prospectors, August Rische and George Hook, returned to the Tabor store. They now needed shovels and blasting powder. This time they got about fifty dollars worth of supplies. At long last, Tabor was in luck. In May, the two prospectors struck it rich at the Little Pittsburg silver mine. Tabor joined his partners with pick and shovel and helped dig out the first wagonload of carbonate ore. Over the next fifteen months, Tabor's share in the mine brought him half a million dollars. With his money, Tabor bought the Chrysolite Mine, which also made him a lot of money. Tabor was suddenly a well known and wealthy man.

In the fall of 1878, Tabor was elected lieutenant governor of the state of Colorado. He moved his family to Denver and in January 1879 bought a house at Seventeenth and Broadway. While Augusta, somewhat unwillingly, settled into her new home and sedate Denver society, Tabor spent more and more of his evenings in variety halls. Newspaper accounts talked of his extravagant gifts and trips with several different women. Among those named were Alice Morgan from the Grand Central Variety Hall in Leadville and Willie Diville from Chicago.

Meanwhile, Tabor kept up with his mining pursuits. He sold his interest in the Little Pittsburg in 1879 to Jerome Chaffee and David Moffat for a million dollars and bought the Matchless Mine for $117,000. He also bought eight hundred shares of stock in the First National Bank of Denver.

Tabor, along with his friend Bill Bush, then began building the Tabor Opera House in Leadville. It was connected by a covered passageway to the Clarendon Hotel next door. Tabor had a bachelor suite on the second floor of the Opera House and stayed there most of the time while Augusta remained in Denver.

After years of moving about, prospecting, running stores, and selling baked goods, Augusta and Horace Tabor were finally rich. It could have been a time to enjoy life. But it did not work out that way. Horace and Augusta quarreled often. Augusta was a homebody. Her husband wanted excitement and night life. Horace was unhappy in his marriage, and he had an eye for lovely, younger women. He was about to meet Elizabeth Doe.

Elizabeth and Harvey Doe had married in Oshkosh, Wisconsin. Their families had recently suffered financial losses, and news of the fortunes being made in the mining camps of the West reached them. Elizabeth Doe, her husband, and her father-in-law headed out to Central City. They located a cabin, settled in, and the men began prospecting. Before long, the men in the mining camp referred to the beautiful new woman in town as "Baby Doe," and the name stuck. Baby Doe's husband and father did not make the fabulous find they'd hoped for. Doe senior gave up and moved to Denver. Harvey Doe made a living as a miner.

Tabor, now a wealthy man and an influential one in state politics, was known for being out in society and enjoying himself. When the governor was away, Tabor, as lieutenant governor, ran affairs of state in Denver. He still found time, however, to make frequent trips to Leadville and lead an active nightlife there.

Baby Doe meanwhile had found little to occupy her in Central City. Bored, she decided to take an excursion to Leadville, hoping there might be more excitement there. She stayed at the Clarendon Hotel, next door to the Tabor Opera House, and she managed to see and meet Horace Tabor. He admired her beauty; she admired his position. It did not take her long to decide that this wealthy man was for her. The two began seeing each other regularly, and soon Baby Doe started divorce proceedings. She was quickly free of Harvey Doe, but Tabor was far from free of Augusta. Tabor set up Baby Doe in a fancy hotel suite in Denver.

In 1880, Horace moved out of the mansion that he had shared with his wife and son in Denver and moved into a suite of rooms at the Windsor Hotel where he was part owner. By this time, the papers were filled with gossip about him, and Augusta knew what was going on, though she was helpless to do anything about it. In December Augusta used some of her money to buy a third interest in the Windsor Hotel. Perhaps part of the reason for this investment was that as an owner, she could keep an eye on her husband. She was determined to remain married to him.

Tabor decided to build a grand opera house in Denver. He bought almost an entire square block of land and set aside $1 million to spend on it. Tabor never bothered to mention this to his wife, who said she first heard about the plan when she read about it in the newspaper. Augusta went off on a trip to Europe. The opera house soon took shape and was almost finished by the time she returned.

All the woodwork in the interior was cherry, and pillars had been imported from Japan. There were stained glass windows and thick, crimson carpet. Six fashion boxes were put in place, and Tabor claimed Box A for himself. On opening night, Tabor gave a short speech from the stage. It was rumored that Baby Doe, veiled, sat in the orchestra circle. Maxey, Tabor's son, sat in Box H with the young woman he would soon marry. But Box A was empty, and Augusta sat at home.

Augusta and Tabor had been together for twenty-seven years. Now Tabor asked for a divorce and also asked to buy Augusta's shares in the Windsor Hotel. Augusta said no to both offers. Although Augusta was not yet officially divorced, she felt abandoned and brought a suit against her husband for alimony. The suit brought about a lot of bad publicity for Horace before it was thrown out of court as illegal. In May of 1882, Augusta sold her interest in the Windsor Hotel and gave her husband a divorce in exchange for about $300,000 worth of property.

Baby Doe was now eager to marry Tabor, but he wanted to wait until he had secured a senate seat and could hold a grand wedding in Washington. He finally agreed that that they could secretly be married but live in separate homes in Denver. In September a justice of the peace married Tabor and Baby Doe in an attorney's office. The license was dated September 30, 1882.

Deciding who would be the next senator from Colorado was complicated. Governor Pitkin was interested in the position himself. One idea was that he would resign as governor, H.A.W. Tabor would become governor, and then Tabor would appoint Pitkin to temporarily hold the senator position until the legislature had time to vote someone in. That would put Pitkin in a good position to be elected to the six-year senate seat. This did not happen, perhaps because Tabor wanted the senate seat for himself.

Many other candidates stood in line for both the short term appointment to finish out Teller's term of office and for the new six-year senate seat. In fact it took eleven caucus votes before a decision was finally made. Once the Colorado legislature voted to give Tabor the short-term senate seat, Tabor went to Washington, and the plans for the elaborate wedding moved forward. Augusta, even at this late date, seemed to think that her husband would return to her after his short stint in the Senate.

The news of the Washington wedding was in all the newspapers. When word leaked out that Baby Doe and Tabor had been secretly married several months earlier, the priest who performed the Washington wedding professed that all this information had been kept from him. He returned the fee the senator had given him and apologized to the archbishop.

On their return to Denver, Baby Doe received no invitations to go out among polite society. Augusta, on the other hand, continued to be invited to every affair, but declined. Tabor, ignoring any warnings of financial problems ahead, kept spending money. He bought an interest in a hotel in New York. He bought acres in Texas where he hoped to succeed in a copper mine. He made mining investments in Mexico. He bought a mansion in Denver for Baby Doe, and he continued to make substantial political contributions. Baby Doe gave birth to her first child, Elizabeth Pearl. Five years later, a second daughter, Silver Dollar, was born to them.

Augusta, meantime, wisely invested the money from her divorce settlement and tripled it well before the economic crash that occurred when Congress repealed the Sherman Silver Act and the government no longer purchased large amounts of silver every month. As a result of the repeal, prices for silver dropped so low that mines could not operate at a profit. Augusta left Denver and retired to Pasadena, California. She died there and left her fortune to Maxey. She also left a diary of her pioneering days with Tabor.

With the repeal of the Sherman Silver Act, Tabor's many mine holdings were suddenly almost worthless. His magnificent empire collapsed. He lost his mines, his other properties, and his Denver mansion. His foreign mining investments did not work out either. By 1897, Horace and Baby Doe were living in poverty. Tabor was broke and was grateful when an old friend arranged to give him a job as postmaster in Denver on January 13, 1898. He served as postmaster until his death on April 10, 1899, from appendicitis.

Tabor's funeral was an elaborate event that he would have loved. Flags hung at half-mast. Telegrams arrived for Baby Doe from all over the world. The body was taken to the capital to rest and under a guard of four soldiers. Services were held in the Capitol followed by a parade of soldiers, police, firemen, and bands. An estimated ten thousand people gathered to watch the cortege.

Baby Doe and her two daughters, ages fifteen and nine, eventually moved back to Leadville. They lived in a shack at the back of the Matchless Mine. The daughters finally left Colorado, but Baby Doe remained at the Matchless Mine until her death. Her body was discovered in the mining shack on March 7, 1935. Baby Doe was buried next to her husband in Denver.

Horace Tabor had become a millionaire. He made his fortune through good luck, some skill, and through the industrious support of his first wife, Augusta. When riches came at last, the Silver King abandoned his old wife. He used his wealth to buy a short-term senate seat—not to serve his state and country, but for self-aggrandizement and to stage an extravagant Washington wedding to establish Baby Doe as his new Silver Queen. In the end H. A. W. Tabor died in relative poverty, leaving behind a legacy of jerklike behavior.

Sources

Bancroft, Caroline. *Augusta Tabor: Her Side of the Scandal.* Boulder, CO: Johnson Publishing Co., 1961.

———. *Tabor's Matchless Mine and Lusty Leadville.* Boulder, CO: Johnson Publishing Co., 1960.

Dumett, Raymond E., ed. *Mining Tycoons in the Age of Empire, 1870–1945.* Burlington, VT: Ashgate Publishing Co., 2009.

Johnson, Marilynn S. *Violence in the West.* Boston: Bedford/St. Martin's, 2009.

Karsner, David. *Silver Dollar: The Story of the Tabors.* New York: Crown Publishers, 1932.

Obmascik, Mark. *Halfway to Heaven.* New York: Free Press, 2009.

Smith, Duane A. *Horace Tabor: His Life and the Legend.* Niwot, CO: University Press of Colorado, 1989.

Smith, Phyllis. *Once a Coal Miner. The Story of Colorado's Northern Coal Field.* Boulder, CO: Pruett Publishing, 1989.

Williamson, Ruby G. *From Kansas to the Matchless: A Tabor Story 1857–1880.* Gunnison, CO: B & B Printers, 1975.

Wood, Richard E. *Here Lies Colorado: Fascinating Figures in Colorado History.* Helena, MT: Farcountry Press, 2005.

Soapy Smith
COURTESY DENVER PUBLIC LIBRARY, WESTERN HISTORY COLLECTION

CHAPTER 9
Soapy Smith

CON MAN OF THE WEST

*I*n the last half of the 1880s, western mining camps and growing cities were filled with all sorts of people. Some were residents and honest merchants. Others were wealthy small town visitors passing through, looking for some fun in the city and often carrying large sums of cash. And some were con men who had devised dozens of ways of parting men from their money. Certainly the most notorious of all these con men was Jefferson Randolph Smith, often called Soapy Smith.

Soapy Smith was a great speaker. He could tell charming and entertaining stories at a respectable dinner party. He could eloquently defend himself in a court of law. He was also a clever con man who could gather a crowd around him on the sidewalk and entice them to bet on which of three walnut shells covered the pea he had hidden right before their eyes. Soapy Smith had the ability to get other con men to join his "organization" and benefit from his protection through contacts with city hall in exchange for paying him a percentage of their profits.

Soapy Smith was at his best as a con man, but he also was known to be handy with a gun, to salt and sell worthless mine property, and to forge checks. In many of his dealings, he proved himself to be a jerk.

A crowd quickly gathered on a sidewalk in the bustling city of Denver in 1881. All eyes were on the bearded man who bantered easily with the crowd. Sometimes he would make them laugh, and at other times he hurled an insult, suggesting that everyone there could certainly benefit from a good scrubbing with his high quality soap. Then he appealed to gambling spirits and greed by pointing out that he was wrapping some of these bars of soap in twenty and one hundred dollar bills before wrapping them again in newspaper for sale. Who would be the lucky one to pay five dollars for a bar of soap and walk away with a hundred dollar bill?

When someone stepped forward to try his luck, pay his five dollars, and unwrap the soap, the people crowded around. When the buyer showed that his soap was wrapped in a twenty dollar bill, more eager customers pushed forward. If interest waned after a while, the seller pointed out that his pile of soap was now small and that no one as yet had claimed the bar wrapped in a hundred dollar bill. More customers decided to buy.

No one in the crowd guessed that those customers who had been "lucky" enough to have picked out a bar of soap with money attached were in the employ of Soapy Smith, the bearded soap seller in front of them and the best con man in Denver.

Jefferson Randolph Smith grew up in Georgia and as a boy worked on the family farm. His father was an attorney whose lack of success may have been due to his bad drinking habit. The senior Smith moved his family to Round Rock, Texas, around 1876, but his law practice did not flourish there either. Jefferson Smith had some knowledge of the Bible and literature, and could charm people with the stories he told. His mother held out hope that her son might become a preacher. The boy, however, was interested in a career that would provide him with money.

Young Jefferson Smith sought employment. He became a delivery boy for a store and a runner for a hotel. One of his jobs was to meet trains and to steer people to the places of business of his employers. Since he was living in Texas, it was natural that the boy also learned to ride and shoot. These skills stood him in good stead when, while still in his teens, he left Texas to help herd cattle on the Chisholm Trail. He served as a "nighthawk," to watch over the herd during the night and bring in the horses early in the morning.

On the trail, Smith made a friend of Joe Simmons. The two young men went back and forth from the trail towns of Kansas to San Antonio and Houston. When possible, Smith stopped in to see his family. Although he continued to work as a cowboy, he spent a lot of his free time at the poker table playing faro. He often gambled all night, and he usually lost. It is reported that Smith often tried to make his fellow gamblers nervous by humming the Sunday school hymn, "Jesus Wants Me for a Sunbeam," as he played his hands.

Jefferson Smith finally said good-bye to his friend and to his cowboy days and rode off to Leadville, Colorado. In the town was a man named Taylor who practiced a shell game. The man used three walnut shells and a small green pea. He challenged the crowd that gathered 'round to guess under which shell the pea would be found. Before long, Smith, a young man in his late teens, was working for the old pro. He would help collect the crowd, or he would place himself in the crowd and pretend to bet and win, encouraging others to give it a try. At the end of the day, Smith would be paid ten dollars.

More important than the money he earned were the lessons he learned from the old pro. He learned to press the pea under the rim of the walnut shell where it wouldn't be seen, so any shell the customer pointed to could be turned over, and the customer always lost. When the shell game seemed to have run its course, Taylor taught Smith a new con using bars of soap. He would take some cakes of soap, wrap real money around some of them, and then wrap them up in newspaper. Customers would pay five dollars for a cake of soap. The "lucky" one would get a cake of soap wrapped in a hundred or ten dollar bill.

As a planted customer, Smith would pay for a bar of soap, picking the one where he could see the edge of a hundred dollar bill, and then run up and down the street, telling everyone of his good fortune and drumming up business for Taylor. His percentage of the daily take soon allowed Smith to move into the Grand Hotel. A dutiful son, he still kept in touch with his mother, often sending her telegrams and money.

You can't stay in the same town for too long using your shell and soap cons. Before long, Taylor left for Minneapolis, and Smith went off to Denver. Soon the young man was expertly performing his con on the streets of Denver. He operated from a wagon pulled by a team of horses. Like many grifters, he was sometimes arrested by the police. It apparently was one of these policemen who booked him, not as Jefferson Randolph Smith, but as "Soapy Smith," and the nickname stuck.

Smith tried to make himself look older and more respectable by growing a heavy black beard and by wearing a black suit. He often wore a diamond stickpin and sported a heavy gold watch chain across his vest. He looked like a prosperous gentleman.

Now it was Soapy Smith who hired shills to stand in the audience and help pull off his con. He met a lot of other pros in Denver such as "Doc" Bagg and "Canada" Bill and learned from them. Bagg would sometimes sell "gold" bricks to bankers, and Canada Bill worked his con games on railroad trips wearing a variety of disguises. Soapy Smith was ready to expand his business.

Smith opened up an office at Seventeenth and Larimer in Denver. He furnished it quite lavishly. He held meetings with fellow con men and sometimes brought in a small group of suckers for a game of cards here. His office had secret exits that could be used when necessary. It didn't take long for a number of the city's con men to become part of his organization. They held allegiance to Soapy Smith, and he bailed them out when they were in trouble. Many of them operated in the Windsor Hotel, which was always filled with wealthy people, or in the Arcade on Larimer Street, which had a gambling room above a restaurant. The Arcade was open day and night, and it was a favorite spot for Soapy Smith to try his hand at winning at the faro table.

Soon more and more con men were part of Soapy Smith's business organization, depending on him to help with steering business their way and to come to the rescue when they got in trouble. Smith made friends with the police and with important politicians who could be paid to look the other way. Things might have continued to go very well if he had stuck to simple con men, but he began to include burglars and stickup men in his group.

At a dance hall one night, Soapy Smith met a singer named Anna Nielsen. He called her Addie. Smith married Addie and bought her a home on Seventeenth Street in Denver. They had three children. Smith told few people of his marriage and kept his business life and his private life entirely separate. He made sure that his children had nothing to do with the underworld, and they grew up to be respected citizens.

Soapy Smith continued to make the bulk of his money from a variety of con games, including selling his bars of soap. When he decided to leave Denver in 1886, the Denver *Herald*, happy to see him go, carried an item that read, "He will give away samples of Denver's best soap and new, crisp fifty dollar bills among his friends at Saratoga, Long Branch, Coney Island, Brighton Beach, and other health and pleasure resorts."

Soapy Smith's "vacation" to the East Coast didn't last long, and he was soon back in Denver. He had added a new skill to his repertoire—forgery. It quickly got him in trouble. At one of his poker games, a player lost at cards and paid his debt by making out a check to Soapy Smith for twenty-nine dollars. The card player went back to Rawlins, Wyoming. Soon he learned that the check he had written had been altered to read one thousand and twenty-nine dollars. The card player, named Blair, took the train back to Denver and swore out a warrant against Soapy Smith for forgery. When the matter came to court, Blair did not appear, and Soapy Smith went free. It was probably one of a number of times that Smith paid up rather than cause himself a lot of grief.

Soapy Smith often carried a gun, a knife, and sometimes a cane. One night, he was playing and losing heavily in a faro game. Always unwilling to quit, even when he was losing, Smith pledged his watch so that he could play one more hand. This time Lady Luck was with him and he won. When he took a hundred dollars from his winnings to redeem his watch, the faro dealer refused. Smith whipped out his knife and held it to the faro dealer's throat until he had a change of heart.

Soapy Smith wanted to stay in Denver because he had a wife and family in the city. He knew that if you wanted to stay in one town, you practiced your cons on visitors, not the locals. If you wanted to be in his organization, you agreed to this approach. One of the best places to find strangers to fleece was at the train station.

This led to the development of a con known as the Bandit Barbers. Prosperous-looking men who got off the train in Denver, tired and dusty, were met by eager young men who gave them a card to go to a barbershop that provided a shave and haircut at very low prices. The visitors, looking for a bargain, went to the shop, and everything looked fine. They climbed in a chair for a haircut and shave. But that was not the end of it; far from it. After the basics were done, the sturdily built barber insisted that the customer also needed a shampoo, moustache trim, dandruff treatment, etc. The customer could protest all he wanted, he still got the full treatment and paid a large sum for it. In addition, if the barber thought this customer was a particularly good prospect with a lot of money, he would cut a small inverted V in the back of the customer's hair. This designated him as an easy mark for other con artists in the organization. Of course Smith got a percentage of the profits from the Bandit Barbers.

Logan Park in Denver was a quiet spot inhabited by families, including Soapy Smith's own respectable wife and children. Then one day a flock of the city's con men descended in force on the park. Someone felt cheated by one of the cons, fists flew, and soon a riot was in full force. The next day's newspapers began a tirade against Soapy Smith, who actually had no part in the event. Since the uproar over the criminal element spilling over into the park was so loud, Smith decided it would be smart to move out of town for a while. He went to visit his family who were vacationing at Steamboat Springs.

His wife and children had been enjoying their pleasant vacation, but the uproar continued in the paper, and this time his family was discussed in the article, along with the news that Soapy

Smith was visiting them. The friendly climate at the hotel changed. Other guests now avoided Smith's wife. Mrs. Addie Smith was terribly upset and left immediately to return to Denver.

Furious that the *News* had openly discussed his family and violated what he thought was an understanding, Smith rushed back to Denver seeking revenge. With one of his cohorts, Banjo Parker, Soapy Smith waited outside the paper's office until he saw Colonel John Atkins, president of the News Printing Company and manager of the paper, come outside to call a cab. Using his cane, Smith beat Colonel Atkins so badly that he cracked his skull. While this was going on, Banjo Parker made sure no one else came to help or join in the fight. Later that evening, the police picked up Smith in a saloon and arrested him. At the jail, he was immediately released on bond.

The next issue of the *News* carried the headline "Soapy the Assassin," and the event was reported as an attempted murder. Six days later, there was a preliminary hearing. Soapy Smith spoke in his own defense. He insisted that he had not been part of the Logan Park riots, and that he had visited Colonel Atkins to talk with him about the charges he had made in his newspaper. Smith said they had reached an understanding and had parted amiably with Smith giving the colonel a cigar. When the latest newspaper attack brought his family into the matter, Smith said he fought Atkins as any man might in defense of his family. Smith's attorney insisted this was not an attempted murder. Soapy Smith was charged with assault and released on one thousand dollars bail.

Soapy Smith decided this might be a good time to leave Denver and go west for a while. He sent his wife and children to St. Louis where they would be away from any further publicity. News of his problems in Denver had spread, however, and Smith found he was not welcome in Cheyenne, Wyoming. He went on to Salt Lake City and then from there to Idaho.

In Pocatello, Idaho, a local con man who did not want competition challenged Smith and ordered him to leave town. Smith drew his gun and there was an exchange of fire. The other man was shot in the leg, and Soapy Smith was taken to jail. He was acquitted of any charge, however, by pleading self-defense. Before long, Smith returned to Denver where efforts at reform had calmed down. He never came to trial on the Idaho assault charge.

Soapy Smith opened the Tivoli Saloon and Gambling Hall. The gambling rooms were on the second floor. Smith was soon making large profits and living lavishly again. He was not happy, however, for his wife and children remained in St. Louis. Soapy Smith seemed more quarrelsome than before and managed to get into several fights. A man came after Smith in a saloon and knocked him down. Smith shot the man in the shoulder. Three weeks later, Smith shot at another man, who ran away after trying to get back money he lost at the gaming tables. Soapy Smith was making news again, and his friends advised him to let up.

Smith continued to make money at the Tivoli and through his thriving con games throughout the city, although more complaints were now regularly being made to the police. Smith decided to move again, this time to visit a Colorado mining town.

Smith moved to Creede, Colorado, around 1891. He liked it and sent for a few of his associates to join him so that they could set up his soap and shell games in the town. He also met with local citizens of Creede and volunteered to help them establish some sort of government. He promised to control the tough element in the community. He installed as town marshal his brother-in-law, John Light. It didn't take long for Soapy Smith to control the town. He kept violence to a minimum. If there were too many problems, Smith put on a marshal's badge himself and assisted his brother-in-law. For a mining town, it was relatively calm. Only once did Marshal John Light have to shoot a man, and that upset him so much that it caused him to resign and leave.

One of the men in Creede who had arrived earlier than Soapy Smith was Bob Ford. Ford owned a saloon and was famous as the man who had shot Jesse James. One day a stranger by the name of Ed Kelly rode into town. Kelly said he was looking for Ford, who wasn't around. Kelly got in a fight over a poker game and was ordered out of town. Instead of leaving town, Kelly waited until evening when he saw Bob Ford walk into a saloon. Kelly followed him and used a shotgun to kill Ford.

An angry mob formed, and it looked as if Kelly would be hung. Calming the crowd and demanding that the law be allowed to take its course was the persuasive Soapy Smith. Ed Kelly was tried, given a life sentence that was later reduced to eighteen years, and was finally given a full pardon due to powerful friends of the Jesse James gang.

The railroad finally reached Creede, and Soapy Smith and his friends frequently made trips back and forth from Creede to Denver. Smith decided it was time to leave Creede permanently and return to his business operations in Denver. Before leaving, he pulled one last con. He salted a mining claim, placing a little gold there for prospective buyers to find. Then he sold the claim to two Easterners for $2,500, and quickly left town before they found out the mine was actually worthless.

Soapy Smith was soon back on his game at the Tivoli. Years before, Smith had a run-in with a man who was connected with the Glasson Detective Agency of Denver. The two men had gotten into a bad fight. Shortly after Smith returned to Denver, he discovered that he and his cohorts were being followed by detectives. Smith wouldn't tolerate that and he wanted to put a quick end to it. An incident occurred that served his purpose. A young woman who was suspected of burglary claimed to have been roughed up by detectives from the Glasson Agency. It made the news, and Smith decided to capitalize on it. He gathered some of his crew, raided the detective agency, beat up the men, and burned their records. The public supported Smith and his men for "fighting for the innocent girl," and soon after, the detective agency closed.

In 1894, Smith and his friends had a bad year. Silver was demonetized, and the economy was very unsettled. There were violent labor strikes in Cripple Creek. The new governor of Colorado was calling for the end of lawlessness and vice. The police and fire commissioners of Denver were removed from office. It was feared that the new group of officials would be very hard on Soapy Smith and his friends. This caused Smith and his buddies to become involved in what was called the City Hall War. They resisted the proposed changes in government, stationed men in city hall, and even threatened to blow it up.

Governor Waite called out the militia, complete with Gatling guns. Soapy Smith, now suddenly called Colonel Smith, still refused to vacate city hall. The military said they would not fire on civilians without direct orders from the governor. In the end, the governor did not give the orders. The military moved back to camp, Colonel Smith and his men vacated city hall, and it proved to be a bloodless war after all.

All these events were enough to convince Soapy Smith that it was time to leave Denver again. He went first to St. Louis to visit his family, and then on to New Orleans. He no sooner arrived in New Orleans than he got in a brawl and was asked to leave the city, so he returned to Denver. There he quickly got into trouble again by assaulting a city detective. The police began cracking down hard on Soapy Smith and his front men. When four con men were arrested, Smith managed to get them out of jail on bond only by agreeing that they would leave the city.

Apparently Smith, who had made himself a colonel during the City Hall War, decided it might be lucrative to keep the title. He had papers forged giving him the commission as colonel and stating that he was a distinguished American military commander.

Using these forged papers, Smith then wrote to President Porfirio Diaz in Mexico stating that he and some trained men would be happy to come down and help with the guerilla warfare problems the president was facing. Smith was invited to come to Mexico City to discuss the matter. Smith was wined and dined. He explained that he had troops ready but not equipped. He felt sure the president would give him $80,000 for his services and to equip his men. The not-so-gullible president advanced $2,000, but sent some men to check up on Smith. When they learned who he really was, the deal was called off.

Soapy Smith then moved about, going first to Houston, then to San Francisco, and finally to Washington, D.C., where he visited a cousin who worked in the government. Smith expressed interest in opening a hotel in Alaska. After enjoying a splendid month of living the high life in Washington, it looked as if Soapy Smith might give up the con artist life. He seemed genuinely interested in taking his family and moving to Alaska to open a legitimate business there. Perhaps that was another con, for he didn't follow through.

Instead, Smith chose to go back to his cohorts in Denver. Met by his friends, Smith announced that he and two of his closest friends would be leaving Denver immediately and would be going to Japan. Puzzled people bid them farewell. As usual, the announced journey itself was something of a con. The three men did not go to San Francisco and then sail for Japan. Instead they went to San Francisco and then caught a tramp steamer to Skagway, Alaska, gateway to the newest gold rush. In a valise, Smith carried dice, poker chips, and half shells of English walnuts, as well as a supply of whisky and good cigars.

When Soapy Smith arrived in Skagway in 1897, he found a fairly lawless town that was much to his liking. Soon more of his former Denver gang joined him. He quickly established himself and before long, Smith was running a small saloon on Holly Street. He was also running his various con games. He and his friends were busy swindling a variety of prospectors in 1897 and 1898. As was his usual procedure, Smith worked his way into the city government, promising to control the lawless element and putting officers he could control into power. Soapy Smith's offices were really the city hall of the town.

Then on July 7, 1898, John Douglas Stewart, a miner, came down the White Pass Trail and arrived in Skagway with $2,700 in gold in a pouch. There are many stories about what happened to this gold. Some said it was stolen, others said Stewart lost the money gambling. Whatever happened to it, Stewart wanted it back and he raised such a ruckus that a sort of vigilante committee, which had been long inactive, was called to a meeting.

Although there seemed to be no specific evidence implicating Soapy Smith in this matter, because of his position with the other con men in town, demands were made of Smith by the committee. He was to bring about the return of the gold. Smith refused. A meeting was called at Sperry's warehouse. Smith and several of his men went down to the warehouse and were turned away by two guards, Frank Reid and Charles Singfelder. A scuffle began and Soapy pushed Reid off the sidewalk, but Singfelder stopped Smith from getting into the meeting. Although Smith was stopped, a few of his men did get inside and created a violent disturbance.

Another meeting was called and because of the crowd it was moved from Sylvester Hall to the wharf. Three men, including Frank Reid, were guarding the approach to the dock. Telling his men to stay back, Soapy Smith appeared and tried to force his way into the meeting. Reid challenged him, both men began shooting, and both were hit. Soapy Smith died immediately and Reid died twelve days later in a hospital. At age thirty-eight, Soapy Smith's long career as a con man and a jerk came to an end.

Sources

Clifford, Howard. *The Skagway Story*. Anchorage, AL: Alaska Northwest Publishing Co., 1975.

Collier, William Ross, and Edwin Victor Westrate. *The Reign of Soapy Smith, Monarch of Misrule, in the Last Days of the Old West and the Klondike Gold Rush*. Garden City, NY: Doubleday, Doran & Company, 1935. While this book contains a lot of fictional dialogue, it is also the source of some interesting photographs.

Robertson, Frank G. and Beth Kay Harris. *Soapy Smith, King of the Frontier Con Men*. New York: Hastings House Publishers, 1961.

CHAPTER 10

Queen Ann Bassett

CATTLEWOMAN OF THE WEST

*D*uring the early 1900s in the northwestern portion of Colorado *in an area called Brown's Hole, there was a constant battle between the little ranch owners and what were called cattle barons. The barons wanted to get rid of the small ranchers by almost any means possible. Sometimes they would buy them out. Sometimes they hired a gunman to warn and chase them out, or if necessary, shoot them.*

Standing firm against the cattle barons were the Bassett women. First Elizabeth Bassett and then her daughter, Ann, had refused to be intimidated into selling or leaving. Ann Bassett, however, did not always appear as a blameless defender of the small rancher. She did whatever she thought was necessary, humane or not, legal or not, fair or not, to thwart the powerful cattle barons. In doing so, she was sometimes a jerk.

An eager crowd packed the makeshift courtroom in Craig, Colorado, when a charge of cattle rustling appeared on the docket. It was not that cattle rustling was so unusual. This crowd had assembled because the defendant was Ann Bassett, quickly named by reporters covering the trial as "Queen Ann." Most of the people in the courtroom that day in 1911, whether friend or foe, would privately agree that she had rustled more than a few cattle in her day, but she had never been caught until now. She was far too smart for that. Had she become careless or unlucky? Or had the evidence presented at trial today been planted by a cattle baron to get rid of her? Would the Queen be convicted on a trumped-up charge?

Brown's Hole, also known as Brown's Park, is located in extreme northwestern Colorado. For the most part it is a desolate

Ann Bassett
COURTESY COLORADO HISTORICAL SOCIETY

area with a few clusters of cedar and sagebrush. But in the early years of ranching in Colorado, Brown's Hole had a singular attraction for some people. The little valley, thirty-six miles long and roughly six miles wide, is hidden from the rest of the world by cliff walls that rise a thousand feet. Flowing through the valley is a river that cuts its way through one of the cliff walls. The only easy access to the valley is from the east, not far from an area called Powder Springs. This was a stopping place frequently used by outlaws on the run, because it was so close to the borders of Colorado, Utah, and Wyoming. Outlaws being pursued by posses could quickly ride across a state line.

Before settlers and outlaws, Native Americans had camped in the valley in summer, and trappers and traders had passed through on their journeys to sell and trade goods. A few pioneers had also come that way. One day, an unlikely rancher and his family arrived. Herb Bassett settled on a parcel of land in Brown's Hole.

Although Herb Bassett worked hard to establish this ranch and provide for his family, he was not a devoted cattle rancher. In fact ranching was foreign to his nature and training. He had been born in New York and grew up in Illinois. Herb was working as a school teacher when he left home to fight in the Civil War. As a musician, he was assigned to the Company K band of the 106th Regiment of Lincoln's Brigade.

At the end of the war, Herb Bassett was mustered out of the army in Arkansas. He chose to stay there and became clerk of the court. In his middle-age, he surprised everyone by marrying a vivacious teenage orphan, Mary Eliza (Elizabeth) Miller, who had been raised by her grandparents. When Bassett lost his clerk's job, the couple decided to move west. They were somewhat uncertain of a destination, but it seemed that California might be their goal. By this time they had two children, and a third child was on the way.

The Bassetts stopped in Green River City, Wyoming, for a brief reunion with Herb's brother Sam, who rode up to see them and invited them to come to his place in Brown's Hole, Colorado, about eighty miles south. Herb decided, however, to stay in Wyoming. For one term, he took a position as a teacher in Evanston. Hoping to carve out a totally new life, he then decided to take his brother up on the offer to go to Brown's Hole. He and his family went there by wagon in the spring of 1878 with plans to ranch in the area. Shortly after they arrived, a second daughter, Ann, was born. According to available records, Ann Bassett was the first white child born in this remote section of Colorado.

The Bassetts had a sprawling ranch that straddled pieces of Colorado, Wyoming, and Utah. Although his background as a teacher and musician had not prepared him for this kind of life, Herb Bassett did what was needed to establish the new ranch. He built a corral and a cabin for his family. He piped in spring water that was used in the house and also to irrigate crops. He established a good hayfield and planted an apple orchard. At least in one way, he was also an innovator. Herb Basset was the first man in the area to fence his property with four-strand barbed wire.

It was Elizabeth Bassett, however, who truly loved the cattle ranch. Much younger than her husband, and with a totally different disposition, she was always riding side-saddle over their land. She would take salt blocks out to the herd, and she was the one who moved the cattle from one pasture area to another. Since she was out on the range, she often came across "stray" calves. It didn't matter from which cattle baron's herd the strays had roamed, she would take them home. Unhesitatingly, she would brand these cattle and add them to her own herd. Sometimes a full grown cow would happen by. Elizabeth Bassett didn't mind killing such an animal and serving the meat to her family. She did whatever she felt was necessary to survive.

Ann and her sister, Josie, grew up on the ranch and learned to ride and shoot. As other siblings came along, it was Josie who stayed home to care for the young ones, while Ann went out riding with her mother and the hired hands.

Because of its location, the Bassett property was the first seen by riders who entered the Brown's Hole area, so the Bassetts had many guests. Such guests were always welcomed, fed, and housed. Several of these visitors chose to stay on and work for the Bassetts. Among these were Isom Dart and Matt Rasch. Dart had spent his early years in Mexico, and it was rumored that he had stolen horses and sold them in Texas. He knew a lot about horses and cattle and became devoted to Elizabeth Bassett. Rasch had been hired to drive some cattle into the area, and he decided to remain. He built a cabin just a couple of miles west of the Bassett house.

As the area grew, a post office was established in 1890. Herb Bassett became the first postmaster. This occupation seemed much more suited to his temperament and training than did cattle ranching. In time, he built a cabin that served as the Ladore Post Office and Store and spent most of his time there. He also supplemented the Bassett income by applying for and receiving an army pension. At this point, he stopped working on the ranch, leaving it to his wife to manage.

Herb read to his children at home, not only the Bible, but Shakespeare, Emerson, and others from his library of books. He had helped organize a public school shortly after his arrival into Brown's Hole. It was made from an abandoned barn, and although she was slightly underage, he enrolled his daughter, Josie, in the school. It was Herb who partitioned off part of the building, put oil paper on the windows, and built a fireplace. This school was used until a real school building was raised some years later.

The extra army pension money proved helpful to Herb and the family. Some of it was used to send Josie off to a Catholic school in Salt Lake City. In spite of the fact that her entire youth had been spent at the ranch, Josie took to school and got along well with the nuns and fellow students. When her mother died at thirty-seven, Josie made the decision not to return to school but to stay at home and raise the family.

Ann Bassett was sent to the school in Salt Lake City, but she did not like it. At the end of only one year, Ann was sent home with the request that she not come back. Ann's father ignored this request, refused to give up on her schooling, and sent her back to the nuns. In this way Ann Bassett received a fairly substantial education although she came home again as soon as she could. She grew into a young woman who could ride, rope, and shoot, as well as quote Shakespeare.

Josie Bassett married Jim McNight, and she and her husband built a cabin on some land left to her by her uncle, just a short distance away at Beaver Creek. Apparently the marriage was not altogether successful and when her husband decided to move into town and run a saloon, Josie divorced him. Herb Bassett didn't want his daughter living out in the country alone, trying to raise her two children, so he convinced Josie to move to Craig where she opened a hotel. Throughout her life, Josie continued to have bad luck with men. After her fifth divorce before age forty, Josie Bassett ended up in Vernal, Utah, on land that now belongs to Dinosaur National Monument. She lived there for many years and her cabin there still stands.

With her mother dead and her sister gone, Ann became the main figure running the Bassett ranch. Her father had had little to do with it for years, and on the death of his wife, he took the opportunity to quit his job as postmaster and to travel. He went to California and began to make extended stops in old soldiers' homes. Occasionally he would return to Colorado but never for long. Ann and her brothers, Eb and George, ran the ranch along with Matt Rasch, who was hired as manager and in time became engaged to Ann. When Herb Bassett died in 1896, some of the cattle barons in the area made an offer to buy the Bassett ranch, but Ann refused.

Many of these cattle barons had managed to amass large pieces of land. Under the Homestead Act, a man could claim one hundred and sixty acres. But the administration of the Homestead Act was often inept and corrupt. A man could use his relatives, hired hands, or even strangers to homestead adjoining land, which he could then buy and add to his land. In this way, some cattlemen were able to get control of twenty miles of riverbank. Ann Bassett was determined to make her living and spend her life here in Brown's Hole. Her refusal of the offer by the cattle barons to buy her land, and her sometimes violent and high-handed actions as an unfriendly neighbor, made many of the large landowners in the area dislike her. They would have been happy to drive her away and add the Bassett land to their own holdings.

Ann Bassett was determined to stay and fully prepared to fight. She did not always fight fairly. Sometimes a herd of cattle belonging to one of the large ranchers came onto her land, eating her grass. Ann Bassett didn't seek a discussion with the large ranchers on how to solve the problem. She and her men would go out riding at night. They would position themselves and stampede the herd over a cliff to their death. Humane concern for the animals apparently didn't enter her mind.

Like her mother before her, Ann would also take any calves that wandered onto her land, brand them, and add them to her own herd. At other times when steers from Ora Haley's Two-Bar

Ranch came onto her land, she would deliberately herd them right into the Green River to be caught in the current and drowned, or to founder in the mud. What the cattle barons considered outrageous behavior, Ann Bassett thought of as survival techniques.

Among the large cattle owners, she had one particular enemy, Ora Haley. Haley owned the Two-Bar Ranch, adjacent to the Bassett land. Tired of what he considered cattle rustling by Ann Bassett and her men, Haley hired a gunman by the name of Tom Horn. A former Pinkerton detective who had been hired to track down and kill bank robbers, Horn was credited with shooting more than a dozen men between 1890 and 1894. Horn had left the Pinkerton agency and was now available as a hired gun for larger ranchers faced with cattle rustling. Horn was paid five or six hundred dollars for each rustler that he shot.

Using an alias, Tom Horn arrived in Brown's Hole. Although not charged or convicted of the crimes, Tom Horn was widely believed responsible for the shooting deaths of both Isom Dart and Ann Bassett's fiancé, Matt Rasch. It was further believed that Horn was paid for these killings by Ora Haley. There were no witnesses who could positively identify Horn, so the murders of the men remained unsolved.

After Tom Horn shot her fiancé, Ann Bassett maintained a short mourning period before taking fifteen hundred dollars of her own cattle money and buying the Smelter Ranch, up on Douglas Mountain. That gave her a home of her own, and from then on, she divided her time between the Bassett homestead and the Douglas ranch.

Since her foreman had been killed, Ann hired a new foreman, Tom Yarberry. Ann then closed off the water hole on Douglas Mountain to all cattle except her own, which was her legal right, but which made special problems for Ora Haley's Two-Bar cattle.

Ann was now twenty-six years old, and she seemed deliberately set to find a husband. Her choice was Hi Bernard. Hi was the foreman for Ann Bassett's worst enemy, Ora Haley. Some people thought that Ann wasn't in love, but, like a jerk, chose to marry Hi simply to get even with Haley by luring away his best hired hand.

Bernard was forty-six years old and was described in a report of the marriage that appeared in the local newspaper as having "no equal" in the management of cattle. Hearing of the marriage, Ora Haley promptly fired Hi Bernard. No doubt Ann had counted on this. Without his foreman, coupled with changes in federal land regulation, Haley's ranch quickly went downhill and came close to ruin.

Of course Bernard didn't miss his former employment because he was now busy working on the Douglas ranch and the Bassett homestead. He was even busier when he filed to homestead the land immediately adjacent to Ann's, expanding their property.

Ann Bassett and Hi Bernard formed the Bassett-Bernard Cattle Company. Even in name, Hi Bernard found himself always kept in a secondary position. There was tension between the couple over who was "boss," and they disagreed over the rights of big and small cattle ranchers. After a couple of years, it became clear that the marriage was not destined to last. Perhaps by this time Ann was no longer in love. Perhaps she was content that she had dealt a strong blow against the cattle baron she hated. Probably the split came from a combination of reasons.

In addition to cattle rustling and aggressive action toward the large ranchers' herds, Ann Bassett was also notorious for harboring outlaws at her ranch. One of these groups was the Hole-in-the-Wall Gang or the Wild Bunch. These were men accused of bank heists and train robberies. Among these outlaws were Butch Cassidy and the Sundance Kid.

Both Butch Cassidy and the Sundance Kid were known to have visited the Bassett ranch house and to have their own hideaways in the area where Ann and Josie had visited. Rumors abounded that one or both of the sisters were girlfriends of these outlaws, although the sisters insisted they were simply good friends. Some rumors went so far as to suggest that Ann Bassett sometimes left Brown's Hole to become a member of the gang under the name of Etta Place, and that she actively took part in some of their Texas adventures.

Whatever their personal relationships, Ann Bassett welcomed the outlaws at her ranch and sold them supplies and horses. One of the outlaws who was a frequent visitor to the Bassett ranch was a man called Kid Curry. Curry made a point of riding out to find cowhands who worked for the large ranchers nearby and warn them to leave Ann Bassett and her property alone.

Bill Patton was the new cattle manager who replaced Hi Bernard at the Two-Bar Ranch. In March 1911, Patton sent a stock detective to spy on Ann Bassett's Douglas ranch. The investigator, posing as a prospector, wandered about supposedly looking for rich mining ore. What he was really looking for was any evidence that would point to Ann Bassett illegally taking Ora Haley's cattle.

The investigator found a freshly butchered steer hanging in Ann Bassett's storeroom. He also found the discarded hide of the steer. The investigator reported back to Patton, and the two took the hide to show the sheriff and file a complaint. As a result, Ann Bassett Bernard and her foreman, Tom Yarberry, were indicted for cattle rustling.

The cattle rustling trial of Ann Bassett, held in Craig, Colorado, was long and dramatic. Everyone took sides, and for the most part, the sympathy was with Ann Bassett. Hi Bernard's replacement as foreman on the Two-Bar Ranch, Bill Patton, was not well liked, and Ora Haley was also under suspicion because he was thought of as a nonresident Wyoming cattle baron. The citizens of Craig, determined to see the trial, actually chipped in and rented the opera house so that more people could get in to watch the proceedings. The trial began in August 1911, less than six months after the indictment.

The prosecution stated that Bill Patton and two of his men had examined the hide of a Two-Bar steer. Someone had cut off the brand from the right flank of the animal's hide, but they insisted that the animal was still identifiable as a Two-Bar steer because of the manner in which the cow had been neutered. How did they know Ann Bassett and Tom Yarberry had stolen and killed the steer? A butchered animal was on the Bassett property.

The defense presented quite a different version of the case. They said the steer was from the Bassett ranch. There had been no attempt to hide the animal or the hide, because there was no need. And if a piece of the hide, where a brand might appear, had been cut away, no doubt it was because someone wanted to frame the innocent. Eb Bassett, Ann's brother, testified for the defense.

Hi Bernard came from Denver to testify on behalf of his estranged wife, and he contradicted the testimony that the neutering techniques at the Two-Bar were so distinctive that they could be used to identify cattle. He insisted they were not that unique. A young cowhand also testified that he thought these were trumped-up charges. He had heard Bill Patton speak openly of his dislike of Ann Bassett and his determination to get rid of her.

Finally, Ann Bassett Bernard testified on her own behalf, presenting a picture of an abused and persecuted lady. She wore elegant clothes and had perfectly coiffed rich brown hair, an hourglass figure, and a regal bearing. The reporters, sensing a good story, had arrived on the scene of the cattle rustling trial early on. They quickly dubbed Ann, "Queen Ann." Actually, in their choice of a nickname, the reporters had recognized one of Ann Bassett's failings. She had a way of presenting herself as better than those around her, putting others down and thinking of herself as above the law.

It was a fight with the little rancher against the big cattle barons. Immediately the press was on Queen Ann's side. The first trial ended in a hung jury. The vote had been two for guilty and ten for innocent. A new trial was ordered and the defendants were released on bail.

The retrial was scheduled to occur fairly quickly, but when the date arrived, Ann Bassett Bernard was ill. The trial was postponed until she would be well enough to attend. The second trial finally began in August 1913. By that time, Yarberry had jumped bail and left the area, so Ann was tried alone. One key witness was missing at the second trial. The young man who had testified on Ann's behalf that the Two-Bar foreman had clearly stated he was out to get her had been shot and killed under strange circumstances. It appeared to some that the lawman who, on a trivial excuse, had shot and killed the young cowboy, had a strong connection with Ora Haley.

During the retrial, Ora Haley, as unpopular as ever, took the stand and under questioning stated he had ten thousand head of cattle. Ann Bassett's attorney promptly pointed out that for tax purposes less than four months earlier, Ora Haley had stated he had only five thousand head of cattle. "Did you lie?" the attorney asked. This put Haley in a very bad light.

The jury took only eight hours to deliberate and cleared Ann Bassett Bernard of all charges. When the verdict came in, it was followed by a huge celebration. The *Denver Post* headline read, BUSINESSES CLOSE, BANDS BLARE—TOWN OF CRAIG GOES WILD WITH JOY. Ann Bassett rented the local movie theater and invited everyone to come dance and feast. The small ranchers and their hired hands celebrated in the streets of Craig for days, and the verdict was viewed as a huge victory for the small ranchers.

After divorcing Hi Bernard, Ann Bassett spent the next ten years ranching at Brown's Hole. She married again, this time choosing a cattle rancher named Frank Willis. From all accounts, Willis adored his wife and was able to put up with her sometimes wild and imperious ways. Once he came home drunk and she knocked him out with a frying pan, but he shrugged off the incident.

After her second marriage, Ann Bassett and her husband moved to Leeds, Utah. Every summer, though, Queen Ann returned to Brown's Hole. She continued to do this until her death in Leeds just short of her seventy-eighth birthday in 1956. Near death, Ann Bassett is quoted as saying, "I've done everything they said I did and a helluvalot more."

Ann Bassett thought of herself as superior and not bound by society's conventions and standards of right and wrong. She lived her life as she wished and never seemed to mind that she occasionally overstepped boundaries. Sometimes she was inhumane to animals and imperious in her dealings with others, both enemies and friends. These kinds of actions earned her jerk status.

SOURCES

Burton, Doris Karen. *Queen Ann Bassett*. Vernal, UT: Burton Enterprises, 1992.

McClure, Grace. *The Bassett Women*. Athens, OH: Ohio University Press, 1984. The author of this book draws on interviews she conducted with surviving family, friends, and enemies of the Bassett family.

Monnet, John B., and Michael McCarthy. *Colorado Profiles: Men and Women Who Shaped the Centennial State*. Niwot, CO: University Press of Colorado, 1996. Contains short biographies of several figures who stand out in Colorado history.

Shirley, Gayle C. *More than Petticoats: Remarkable Colorado Women*. Guilford, CT: Globe Pequot Press, 2002. This book profiles fourteen women who were prominent in Colorado history.

CHAPTER 11

Tom Horn

GUN FOR HIRE

*M*ost of the men Tom Horn shot and killed were train robbers *and cattle rustlers. He worked for the Pinkerton Detective Agency handling investigations in Wyoming and Colorado. After 1894 he hired out as a range deputy and U.S. marshal for wealthy ranchers in Colorado and Wyoming. His title may have been "Range Detective," but he was really a killer for hire. In 1900 he was commissioned by various big cattlemen in Wyoming and northwestern Colorado. There he killed two men at Brown's Hole.*

While the two men at Brown's Hole, Matt Rasch and Isom Dart, may have rustled some cattle, it had not been proved against them. By posing as a stranger using an alias, hiding in ambush, and shooting these men for a few hundred dollars, Tom Horn proved himself to be a jerk.

It was a cold crisp October morning in the rangelands of northwestern Colorado in the year 1900. Isom Dart stepped out of the door to his cabin and paused. He and two friends were headed for the horse corral. Before Dart could take more than a few steps, two bullets were fired from someone hiding nearby in the shrubbery. One bullet entered Dart's head, and the other struck him in the chest. He died instantly. Dart's death was remarkably similar to a previous shooting of another small cattle rancher in Brown's Hole, Colorado. Matt Rasch, a friend of Dart's, had been found shot dead in his cabin only three months earlier. No one witnessed that shooting, but both Rasch and Dart were killed with a .30-30 rifle, and the Winchester .30-30 was Tom Horn's favorite weapon. Although the evidence at this point was weak and only circumstantial, there was no doubt in the minds of the Brown's Hole residents: The gunman was Tom Horn.

Tom Horn
COURTESY COLORADO HISTORICAL SOCIETY

Both Rasch and Dart may have been minor thorns in the sides of the Colorado and Wyoming cattle barons who wanted to drive small ranchers out. The biggest sin of these men may have been their close ties to the Bassett family. Elizabeth Bassett was an early homesteader and fearless cattle rancher at Brown's Hole, or what she insisted on calling Brown's Park. The cattle barons hated the Bassetts and what they called the Bassett Gang. It was true that Dart and Rasch, and probably Elizabeth Bassett herself, rustled a few cattle, although that had not been proven against them. In the eyes of the cattle barons, they were a constant source of irritation, because they occupied good land and took up scarce water.

Isom Dart was born into slavery in 1849 in Arkansas where he had the name Nat Huddleston from his owner. As a young man, he was no stranger to law-breaking. Nat Huddleston was sixteen years old when the Civil War ended. He picked up skills in riding and shooting while working on a ranch in Texas before making his way to Mexico. There he joined some bandits in stealing horses and driving them across the Rio Grande into Texas. Before long, he headed up what came to be known as the Tip Gault Gang, specializing in horse stealing. Following the practice of other outlaw gangs who liked an isolated area that was safe from the law, the Tip Gault Gang made Brown's Hole their base camp in northwestern Colorado.

After a horse stealing raid in Wyoming, lawmen gave chase, caught up with, and shot most of Huddleston's gang. Nat Huddleston managed to get away and went to Oklahoma, where he changed his name to Isom Dart. After a time, he returned to Brown's Hole, tried to steal some cattle, got caught, and after this, decided to turn straight. As a law-abiding citizen, he was even elected constable in Sweetwater County, Wyoming, in 1884. He ran a small ranch of his own in Wyoming. He met the Bassetts, successful cattle ranchers in Brown's Hole who had been there since 1878, and developed a friendship with them. Dart was especially devoted to Elizabeth Bassett, who was the force behind the Bassett cattle ranch.

Madison Rasch, Matt for short, supposedly a nephew of Davy Crockett, had come to Brown's Hole in 1882 as a trail boss for the Middlesex Cattle Company from Texas. He stayed on at Brown's Hole, running his own small cattle ranch, and became a close friend of Isom Dart and the Bassetts. He even became engaged to the Bassett's daughter, Ann. Rasch was chosen to be president of the Brown's Park Cattle Association and helped establish and enforce the dividing line on the eastern boundary of land separating the Brown's Park cattle from the herd of cattle baron Ora Haley.

A few cattle ranchers in the area of Brown's Hole had huge holdings in Colorado and Wyoming. Among these cattle barons, as they were called, was Ora Haley. He held enormous holdings and bought up the land on the eastern edge of Brown's Hole. These ranchers with large spreads in the area deeply resented the small holdings of homesteaders who had some of the best pieces of land and thus decreased the amount of water available for the large herds.

Ora Haley, John C. Cobb, and a few other big ranchers in that area met early in 1900 to discuss what might be done about these pesky small ranchers. They were sure that Rasch and others of Bassett's supporters, whom they referred to as the Bassett Gang, were stealing their cattle that wandered from the eastern edge onto the Brown's Hole area. Cobb thought he had a solution. He had met Tom Horn when Horn worked for the Pinkerton Detective Agency. Cobb suggested that they hire Horn and pay him five hundred dollars for each cattle thief that he killed. The others agreed and Tom Horn entered the picture.

In April of 1900, a stranger arrived in Brown's Hole. He called himself Tom Hicks, seemed friendly enough, knew a lot about cattle and horses, and quickly found a job in the area. He went to work for a few weeks as a cook and cowboy for Matt Rasch on his small spread near Lodore Canyon. Most people accepted him readily, but for some reason Ann Bassett regarded him with suspicion. Horn went to work in his usual way. He took his time, got to know people, studied their routines so that he could be confident that he knew when and where they would be doing their normal chores.

It wasn't long after Tom Hicks's arrival that anonymous notes were found tacked up to the doors of small ranchers in the area telling them to leave. Most people ignored these notices. Weeks passed, and nothing unusual happened. Then in July, Matt Rasch was found shot dead in his cabin with two bullets in him. A rumor, probably started by Tom Hicks, circulated suggesting that Isom Dart was the man who had shot Matt Rasch because the two of them had quarreled over Dart's fair share of some rustled cattle. Then three months later, Isom Dart was shot dead as he stepped out of his doorway. Two Bassett men were with him and said they were headed for the corral to saddle their horses when the deadly shot rang out from a clump of bushes nearby where someone had been hiding.

By this time, the stranger Tom Hicks had conveniently left. Ann Bassett and the other residents of Brown's Hole insisted that Hicks was the gunman, Tom Horn, and they denounced him as the murderer of both men. By this time, Tom Horn was reported to be in Dixon, Wyoming. He had cut two new notches on the butt of his Winchester and had a pocket full of bills, but there was no real direct evidence to connect him to the murders. Later, in a letter dated January 1, 1902, Tom Horn wrote about some new rustlers that he was setting out to hunt down, "They can scarcely be worse than the Brown's Hole Gang and I stopped the cow stealing there in one summer." Such bragging dispels any serious doubts that it was Tom Horn, posing as Tom Hicks, who gunned down Dart and Rasch.

Who was this man who so coolly shot and killed so many people for a few hundred dollars? Thomas Horn Jr. was born on November 21, 1860 on a six-hundred-acre farm in Missouri near the towns of Granger and Etna. He was the fifth of twelve children. Young Horn was not interested in farming. At age sixteen, he headed west and hired on as a civilian scout in the U.S. Cavalry. Horn took part in tracking Apaches in the Apache Wars, and he aided in the capture of Geronimo. Horn then hired out as a gun-man in what was known as the Pleasant Valley War in Arizona, a fight between cattlemen and sheep men.

Handy with a gun, Horn was a natural candidate to become a deputy sheriff for a time in Arizona. In addition to being a great shot, he was also known for his tracking skills, and this combination of abilities caught the attention of the Pinkerton Detective Agency. By the early 1890s, he was handling their investigations in both Wyoming and Colorado as well as other western states. He often worked out of the Denver office.

In one of his cases, Horn and another agent captured two men who had robbed the Denver and Rio Grande Railroad in Frémont County, Colorado. He tracked down the notorious robbers Peg-Leg Watson and Red Curtin in Oklahoma. Although he sometimes captured men without firing a shot, he is credited with shooting to death seventeen men during his four years with Pinkerton. Horn is quoted as having said, "Killing men is my specialty; I look at it as a business proposition, and I think I have a corner on the market."

Tom Horn was allowed to retire, under pressure, from the Pinkerton Agency, not because he killed too many people, but as the result of charges that he had robbed a man for cash to settle a gambling debt. The Pinkertons let Horn go rather than take the bad publicity of having one of their own men convicted of robbery and sent to jail. After Horn resigned in 1894, for the next several years he hired out as a range deputy or U.S. marshal for wealthy ranchers in Colorado and Wyoming.

Horn learned that if he simply collected evidence of cattle rustling and brought the thieves in to the authorities, they received very light punishment. Meeting with the cattle owners, Horn suggested that he mete out his own form of punishment—shooting the thieves. Many of the men in the cattlemen's association were opposed to such bloodshed, but other individual cattle barons were ready to pay for Horn's brand of service. Tired of waiting for what they saw as justice, they were ready to become both judge and executioner.

William Lewis, an Englishman, had 160 acres of land right next to that of John C. Coble of the Iron Mountain Cattle Company. Lewis had stolen cattle and openly bragged about it. He also ignored notes, tacked to his door, telling him to leave. One day in 1895 Lewis's body was found. There were no witnesses to the shooting and no clues. The inquest revealed nothing about the identity of the murderer. More notices were sent out and tacked to doors, and this time, several of the small ranchers chose to leave. Others held on. About six weeks later, rancher Fred Powell was shot dead. His land was located about ten miles from Lewis's.

Again the murder was carefully planned and carried out. The assassin clearly knew when Powell would be in an accessible spot. A hired hand, who was a witness to Powell's shooting, said that he was cutting willows when he heard a shot. He never saw the assassin. The witness said the shot came from a ledge of rocks about 250 feet distant.

When Charles Keane received a note a few days later that read, "If you don't leave this country within three days, your life will be taken the same as Powell's was," Keane heeded the message and left.

Horn left his job as range detective to serve in the army during the Spanish-American War, but he contracted a fever and saw little action. Upon leaving the army, Horn returned to the Wyoming/Colorado area, where he went to work for John C. Coble as a hired gun. It was during this time that he shot and killed Matt Rasch and Isom Dart.

Horn was working again near Iron Mountain, Wyoming, for the Iron Mountain Cattle Company in July 1901 when he became involved in his most notorious case. He had stayed with the family of James Miller for two nights before fourteen-year-old Willie Nickell was shot twice and killed. The Nickell family was in a dispute with the Miller family over Nickell's sheep grazing on Miller land. There were many questions over this killing. Some thought that because of the bad blood between the two families, the Millers were responsible for Willie Nickell's death. Others thought Tom

Horn had been hired and knowingly committed the murder. Still others believed that Willie was not the intended victim, but that Tom Horn shot him mistaking the boy for his father. Kels Nickell is quoted as saying, "I think the intention was to get me in place of the boy."

The careful planning that went into the killing of Willie Nickell suggests Tom Horn's involvement. The shooter was concealed in a wall of rocks within range of a gate about three-quarters of a mile from the Nickell household. It was known that Horn always spent time observing and discovering the habits and routines of his victims. By being in a pile of granite rocks near the gate to the road with the early morning sun to his back, the killer would have a perfect shot when the horseman dismounted to unhook the gate loop.

This day, however, did not go in its usual way. Kels Nickell sent his son, Willie, to ride to Iron Mountain Station and bring back a sheepherder to work on their place. Instead of being sunny, it had rained the day before, and on the early morning of the shooting, there was ground fog. Willie wore his father's hat and slicker to keep dry. Dressed in this way, did Tom Horn mistake the boy for his father? Or was it someone else entirely who did the shooting? No one was certain. They knew the time and place of the killing, and they knew it was not accidental, because Willie did not have a gun with him.

Since the Millers and Nickells had been at odds with each other, the first thought was that it was a local killing, the result of a feud. But there was no evidence of any kind. Even after his son was killed, Kels Nickell insisted that he would stay and not be driven away in spite of the fact that he had received an anonymous note telling him to leave.

A week later, on August 4, Kels Nickell was milking a cow about six hundred yards from his house when someone shot at him five times from a concealed spot. The shooter hit Nickell three times but did not kill him. Later that day, seventy-five sheep pastured by Nickell were shot or clubbed to death. The shepherd reported that four masked men had killed them and had threatened him.

Two of Nickell's small children testified that they had seen two men that morning, and that the men had ridden off on a bay and gray horse. Those colors matched horses that Jim Miller owned. Nickell made a statement implicating Miller and his two sons. The three Miller men were arrested peaceably. They furnished evidence of where they were at the time of the shootings and were released. It was decided only that the shootings were the result of the war that was raging between sheep men and cattlemen. The local sheriff was very ill at this time, and he asked Joe LeFors, a deputy U.S. marshal, to keep on the case. Kels Nickell eventually recovered from his wounds, sold his land, and moved to Cheyenne.

It was December 1901 when the coroner's inquest into the death of Willie Nickell finally ended. Still LeFors, who had promised justice to Willie Nickell's mother, did not stop working on the case. Instead, he interviewed a woman who said that Horn had been living at her place near the scene of the killing during the time of the Willie Nickell shooting. She said that she had brought sandwiches to him at his hiding place among the rocks not far from the Nickell gate.

LeFors, on the promise of helping Horn get a new job with a cattleman as a hired gunman, got Horn to come and talk with him. LeFors arranged it so that a law officer and a court stenographer were within earshot of the meeting and that they took down all that Horn said. During the conversation LeFors asked questions about Horn's past exploits and Horn gave some damning details indicating that he had shot the boy.

On the strength of the conversation taken down by the stenographer, Horn was arrested on January 13. On January 24, the preliminary hearing was held. On the basis of LeFors's testimony about the conversation he had held with Tom Horn, Horn was bound over for trial without bail.

With such a dreadful crime and such a well known suspect, it was hard to find a satisfactory jury, but the trial finally began on October 10 in Cheyenne, Wyoming. Witnesses were called and spoke. There was much discussion over whether the bullets that killed Willie Nickell were .30-30 rifle shot, or larger. Tom Horn was finally called to the stand on October 17 when he was interrogated. The next day, he was cross-examined. During cross examination, Tom Horn stated that he was not in the area during either of the Nickell shootings. He said he was one hundred miles away when Kels Nickell was shot.

Horn smoothly tried to explain his responses that the stenographer had taken down, and that appeared to many to be a confession to his crimes. When LeFors had asked where Horn's horse was during the killing of Willie Nickell, Horn had said, "a long ways off." In court, Horn explained that indeed his horse was a long ways off because he was nowhere near that spot. When he'd responded to a question about not leaving tracks by saying that he was careful not to even leave any footprints at the scene, Horn again explained that was true. He couldn't have left footprints, because he wasn't there. Horn explained that when he said the shot was fired from three hundred yards and was the best shot he'd ever made, he was just bluffing and telling LeFors what he wanted to hear.

Was Horn simply spinning tales for an audience, and was he now telling the truth? Horn went on to testify, "As far as actual killing is concerned, I never killed a man in my life or a boy either." Everyone knew that this denial was not the truth. Horn was known for having killed seventeen men while working for the Pinkerton Agency.

One of the greatest shortcomings of Tom Horn's defense was that his attorney never managed to put a witness on the stand who could indicate that there were alternative suspects; others who might have shot Willie Nickell.

The jury took the case at 11:30 in the morning and rendered their verdict at 4:37 in the afternoon. Horn was found guilty of murder in the first degree and sentenced to be hanged. Horn was not granted a new trial, but the case was referred to the supreme court, which stayed the execution until it had time to hear the case. There were rumors of a plot to break Horn out of jail. On August 10, a jailbreak was attempted. Horn and another prisoner managed to escape but were quickly caught and brought back to jail.

On October 1, the Wyoming Supreme Court upheld the lower court's ruling. There was another flurry of activity with a supposed confession by another man and witnesses who now admitted lying at the trial. The only hope now was a petition to the acting governor, Fennimore E. Chatterton, to commute the sentence from death to life imprisonment. Chatterton had assumed the governorship when the elected governor had died in office.

Chatterton received many communications on Tom Horn's behalf and also received a death threat if he did not commute the sentence. Chatterton took time to read the stenographic notes and decided that unless the entire conversation was regarded as a joke, there was no defense. He also reviewed an affidavit from Gwendolene Kummel suggesting that Victor Miller was the killer and that he had admitted as much to her. Three other affidavits also suggested that the Millers were responsible for the shooting.

After looking at many affidavits, the governor made his decision. Horn would hang. Even a week before the date of the execution, John Coble kept writing to Tom Horn that he would never hang.

During the last few days before the execution, troops surrounded the block where the jail and courthouse were located. There was a Gatling gun on the roof.

The date of the hanging was set for November 20, 1903, in Cheyenne, Wyoming. For the first time, a special new contraption called the Julian gallows would be used. In effect the design of the gallows made the condemned man hang himself. When he stepped into place, the weight of the man being hung depressed two levers of a trapdoor and set in motion the series of events resulting in the hanging.

Tom Horn requested that his friends, Charley and Frank Irwin, sing a favorite hymn, "Life's Railway to Heaven," which they did. Thirty-one seconds after being lifted into place, Tom Horn dropped.

Tom Horn's brother Charles arrived and took Horn's body back to Boulder, Colorado, for burial. The funeral expenses were paid for by Tom Horn's old friend and employer, John Coble.

Historians do not agree on whether or not Tom Horn murdered fourteen-year-old Willie Nickell. In a letter written by Tom Horn just a few minutes before his death to his friend John Coble, Horn stated that he did not take part in the killing of Willie Nickell. Whether or not he was involved in shooting the Nickells, Tom Horn is surely the jerk who hid in the bushes outside the cabins of Isom Dart and Matt Rasch in Brown's Hole and murdered them.

SOURCES

Carlson, Chip. *Tom Horn: "Killing Men Is My Specialty . . .": The Definitive History of the Notorious Wyoming Stock Detective.* Cheyenne, WY: Beartooth Corral, 1991.

Carlson, Chip, and Larry D. Ball. *Tom Horn: Blood on the Moon: Dark History of the Murderous Cattle Detective.* Glendo, WY: High Plains Press, 2001.

Krakel, Dean F. *The Saga of Tom Horn.* Lincoln, NE: University of Nebraska Press, 1954.

Monaghan, Jay, and Larry D. Ball. *Tom Horn: Last of the Bad Men.* Lincoln, NE: University of Nebraska Press, 1946.

CHAPTER 12

Jennie Rogers And
Mattie Silks

PISTOL PACKING MADAMS

*D*enver, Colorado, had a large red light district like almost every western town in the late 1880s. Many of the establishments located there were run by madams. Some madams had only one house while others ran several houses of prostitution and leased them to other madams.

Mattie Silks ran brothels in Georgetown, Leadville, and Denver, Colorado, as well as in Dawson City, Alaska. She sold one of the brothels to Jennie Rogers, who, in time, moved to Market Street to set up the most elegant of the Denver brothels, the famous House of Mirrors. Eventually, Mattie Silks bought the House of Mirrors and established herself as Queen of the Red Light District in Denver.

Both Jennie Rogers and Mattie Silks had been known to use pistols now and again when they became jealous over their men. Both frequently had their names in the newspaper for breaking the law. On more than one occasion, Mattie Silks fired off her pistol with intent to kill. Jennie Rogers abetted one of her boyfriends in blackmailing a local influential businessman. Sometimes these feisty women proved that they could be jerks.

Standing on the front porch of the Denver businessman's home was a police officer in uniform with a warrant in hand. The officer explained that he'd received a tip on a cold case and would be searching the man's yard for the buried remains of a murdered woman.

In no time at all, the officer appeared back on the businessman's doorstep with a skull that he said he had found buried in the backyard. Was it from the businessman's first wife who had

Mattie Silks
COURTESY COLORADO HISTORICAL SOCIETY

disappeared mysteriously years before? Even if it proved to have no connection to the former wife, did the businessman want to be booked and investigated, which might put quite a crimp in the man's plans to run for political office? Or would he rather pay $17,000 for silence? If he chose the latter, the officer would forget about finding the skull or filing a report. Not so coincidentally, $17,000 was just the right amount of money needed for Jennie Rogers to buy and remodel a building for her latest luxurious Denver brothel.

The businessman paid up and Jennie Rogers now had the funds she needed to buy a building, remodel it, and open the most famous house of prostitution in Denver: the House of Mirrors. The Denver businessman never ran for political office. No one ever learned what had really happened to his first wife who had mysteriously disappeared, clearing the way for him to marry a divorcee and take over a newspaper. And the businessman never learned that the policeman who stopped at his door wasn't even from Denver but from St. Louis and that the warrant he carried was a fake.

In fact, it was the policeman, a former lover of Jennie Rogers, who had dug up an old skull and some bones from a burial plot and planted them in the businessman's backyard. (Some versions of the story say that it was actually the skull of a Native American woman taken from a raised wooden burial platform.) Wherever the remains came from, and whatever happened to the first wife, Jennie Rogers clearly didn't much care. With the help of her former boyfriend, Rogers had perpetrated a hugely successful scam.

In the late 1880s, many of the large and small western mining towns such as Butte, Montana, and Georgetown, Colorado, held far more men than women. Most of these towns had a red light district, usually unregulated. Famous for its houses of prostitution, Holladay Street in Denver was one of these red light districts. An estimated one thousand prostitutes lived and worked there. Some of these houses were little more than small shacks where one woman plied her trade. Others contained many women, living in large and ornate establishments. These high class brothels were often called boardinghouses, and the women who worked in them were frequently called "boarders." To advertise, the prostitutes dressed in fine clothes and walked or rode discreetly about in open carriages for others to see them. These women often carried poodles. In fact poodles were so associated with prostitutes at the time that other women in town wouldn't think of owning one.

Another means of advertising was through directories that were available in some saloons, restaurants, and hotels. The 1895 *Travelers Night Guide of Colorado* advertised brothels throughout the state along with scenic photographs of mountains and lakes. These small books that could fit in a vest pocket contained the names and addresses of leading parlor houses. Some also contained the names of the girls who worked in them. In Denver many of these parlors were on Holladay Street, later named Market Street.

These expensive parlor houses were located in prime locations and usually had servants and bouncers. They were run by madams who were sophisticated and discreet. Two of the most notorious were Jennie Rogers and Mattie Silks.

Her given name was Leah J. Tehme, but Jennie Rogers, as she was known in Colorado, had run through several names and several husbands before she arrived in Denver in 1880. She had married a doctor in St. Louis and took the name of Leah Fries. Then the story was that she had run off with a Captain Rogers on a Missouri steamship.

A striking-looking woman, Jennie Rogers was a very tall, slender brunette, who almost always wore a pair of emerald earrings. Rogers paid $4,600 for her first parlor house, which she bought from another notorious madam, Mattie Silks, in January 1880. Now and again, her name appeared in the *Rocky Mountain News* in an item about her "unladylike conduct." Jennie loved horses and horseback riding and was known to ride through the streets of Denver, which she thought was a good way to advertise. She met John "Jack" Woods who worked part time at the horse stable, and the two became a couple.

In 1889, after securing $17,000 in her blackmail scam helped by her former police boyfriend from St. Louis, Jennie bought and remodeled a building that became know as the House of Mirrors, located at 1942 Market Street. The building had been remodeled by a well-known architect named William Quale. The exterior gray masonry displayed five stone facial sculptures. The house was filled with polished wood on the walls and ceiling. Oriental carpets covered the floors, and a beautiful crystal chandelier hung from the ceiling. A narrow, walnut-banistered staircase led from the ground floor to the second story. Chairs stood on golden legs, and the divans were richly brocaded. Sometimes music was provided by an orchestra and at other times by a lovely girl playing a harp. Located only a short walk from the Colorado legislative building, this "boardinghouse" had a high-class clientele.

Another Denver madam, Laura Evans, described from memory the large ballroom in the House of Mirrors to western historian Fred Mazzulla:

Directly south of this parlor was the ballroom. There were mirrors about three feet wide that went from the ceiling to the floor. These mirrors were in oval frames. The frames were carved with figures of nude women. There were electric lights all around the ballroom. The five-piece colored orchestra sat on an elevated platform. There were high-backed gothic-style chairs around the room. The chairs had big stuffed arms. There were ottomans on each side of the chairs. The girls were permitted to sit only on the ottomans. They were not permitted to sit on the chairs or on the laps of the gentlemen guests.

Business boomed for Jennie Rogers, and she soon added a passageway from the House of Mirrors to the house next door, which she acquired by buying out a lease. Her boyfriend, Jack, used some of Jennie's money to buy a saloon in Salt Lake City. His business thrived, too. The two of them made frequent visits to see each other. On one occasion when Jennie came to visit unexpectedly, she found another woman with Jack and fired her pistol, wounding him. She was arrested briefly. She and Jack finally married in August of 1890, but eventually separated. Jack died in Omaha, Nebraska, in February 1896.

Part of the time, Jennie Rogers ran her brothel herself, but sometimes she leased it and went traveling. With the large sums of money she made, she also invested in real estate. While on a visit to Boston, she learned that she had Bright's disease, and decided to stay on for a time. She opened a new parlor there and soon came to the attention of a Boston businessman, Archibald Fitzgerald. Two years later in 1904, although Fitzgerald was twenty years her junior, Jennie Rogers married him in Hot Springs, Arkansas.

Jennie Rogers Fitzgerald returned to Denver for the funeral of an old friend. While she was there, she learned that Fitzgerald was still married to another woman and appeared to be only interested in getting his hands on her Denver properties. She left him and hired a divorce attorney, but never actually got a divorce. In 1907 she moved back to Denver for good. She leased her House of Mirrors and moved into a home of her own. Apparently she forgave Fitzgerald, because occasionally she would make short trips with him to Hot Springs.

In 1909, at age sixty-five, she wrote a will, leaving everything she had to her sister, a niece, and a nephew. Shortly after that she died on October 17, 1909. Archibald Fitzgerald challenged her will and eventually settled for some cash, jewelry, and property in Illinois. When her estate was sold, Mattie Silks bought back the House of Mirrors.

Mattie Silks, the so-called Queen of the Red Light District, most likely was born Martha Ann Normann on a small Kansas farm in 1846. (Other records suggest she was born in Terre Haute or Gary, Indiana, in 1848.) She was short, blue-eyed, and blonde. In 1865, when she was around nineteen years old, she was managing a fancy parlor house outside of Springfield, Illinois. Mattie made it clear that she was not a prostitute; she was a businesswoman. She ran a posh parlor house to make money. Mattie dressed in fancy clothes and, whether true or not, she spread the story that her dresses always had two pockets—one in which to carry gold coins and one in which she carried a pistol.

Mattie and her girls moved about quite a bit, to Dodge City, Abilene, and Hays City, Kansas. Forsaking cowboys, she then went north in wagons to mining camps. She set up tents for her girls just downhill from the mining camps and provided luxurious settings within the tents. On one occasion when an epidemic hit the mining camp, Mattie won a lot of good will by using the tents as hospital tents with her girls acting as nurses.

By 1875 she had moved to Georgetown, Colorado, where she soon earned the name of the Silver Queen of the Rockies. While there she met a card player named Silks, may or may not have married him, but at least took his name and used it from then on. (Some historians suggest that there was no man named Silks, and that she coined that name simply because she liked to dress in silk.)

A substantial amount of the silver pulled out of the mines in and near Georgetown was spent in Silks's brothel. It was one of five parlor houses on Brownell Street. An evening with one of her girls would cost a man between ten and two hundred dollars. Mattie kept 40 percent of the money and she provided laundry, room, and board for her girls. The girls, however, had to buy their own clothing, makeup, and perfume, usually billing these to the madam's account, for later repayment. Rather than getting rich, most of the women found themselves often in debt to the madam.

Before long, Mattie Silks was one of the wealthiest women in the trade. A good many men vied for Mattie Silks's attention, but she wasn't interested in the miners or cowboys who made advances to her. Instead she was attracted to a handsome young man named Cortez D. Thompson. He was tall, lean, sandyhaired, and sported a handlebar mustache. Thompson was a former fireman who now was a foot runner who raced men for large sums of money. In a race, he cut quite a dashing figure wearing star-spangled trunks.

Crowds of people came out to watch such races, and the wealthy gambled considerable sums of money on them.

Silks was drawn to the handsome young man and wasn't put off by the fact that he had a wife and child in Texas. Thompson, in turn, liked Mattie's looks, charm, and especially her money, which she gave him freely. In fact, he used her money to buy her a gift—a silver cross studded in diamonds, which she almost always wore.

When Mattie moved to Denver, Cort Thompson came with her. By opening her Denver establishment in 1876, Mattie Silks definitely moved up in the world. She paid $13,000 for a three-story brick building with twenty-seven rooms. Mattie had twelve prostitutes (or boarders) working in her house. She bought or rented space in adjoining buildings and expanded her business. Her main building was fashionably decorated. All clients were expected to be well behaved, and if a man didn't conduct himself well, he was not permitted to enter again.

Mattie's brothel was expensive. She made a lot of money on which she and Thompson lived lavishly. They bought fashionable clothes from Paris and enjoyed good food and expensive wines. Thompson spent a lot of money at the racetrack. Unfortunately Thompson was not content to be a happily kept man. He had affairs with numerous women.

Mattie Silks sometimes was mentioned in the *Rocky Mountain News*. On March 22, 1877, an item in the paper mentioned she had been fined twelve dollars for drunkenness. In August of that year, she went to a picnic and a footrace to see Thompson run. She bet a large sum of money on him, and he won. A fair amount of drinking went on during the celebration. While they were celebrating, Silks got into an argument with another madam, Kate Fulton. It had been rumored that Cort Thompson was seeing Kate Fulton, and Mattie was jealous. From simply hurling words at one another, the fight between the two women escalated to blows. When Kate Fulton hit Mattie Silks, Thompson got into the fight to protect Mattie and struck Kate Fulton. Then Fulton's boyfriend joined the brawl.

According to some versions of this story, that was not the end of the fight. Mattie Silks and Cort Thompson left the area in a carriage. As they drove away, another carriage came up beside theirs, and someone fired a shot at Thompson. Whether or not that happened, it does appear that Mattie called for a duel with Kate Fulton.

The two madams met on Denver's Colfax Avenue. Both fired, and they missed each other. The story of this duel has been greatly embellished over time, with some versions stating that one of the bullets nicked Cort Thompson. That version is supported by an article that appeared in the *Rocky Mountain News* on August 26, 1877, about Mattie Silks and Kate Fulton, describing a "disgraceful row" in which it reports that Thompson received a pistol wound in the neck that was "not regarded as serious."

Whatever else happened, or didn't happen, the fight at the picnic was good publicity for Mattie Silks. It gave her true notoriety, and her business did very well. Mattie and Cort left Denver for a time to visit Kansas City where they spent a lot of time at the Overland Park Race Track.

Silks continued to run her house for twenty years and invested in other small houses, too. It was common at that time for the police to round up and arrest the working girls every now and then. When this happened, the brothels were empty. Rather than endure this, Silks was known to bribe local officials. She soon had good connections, and while other brothels were being raided, Mattie Silks's parlor house was left alone. She knew it was far cheaper to pay bribes than to have her business shut down for several days.

Her business connections paid off in other ways, too. In 1885, Mattie Silks's parlor house was given a liquor license by the city of Denver. It was very rare for this to happen. Most brothels served liquor but they did it illegally. Other rumors circulated that she sometimes traded on her attractiveness. If an important businessman took a special liking to her, Mattie would string him along, trying to persuade him to enter into some business deal that would be of benefit to her local powerful backers. For these "special favors" to potential investors, the local officials were said to have paid off some of Mattie's notes that were outstanding.

When Thompson's wife died, he married Mattie Silks in July 1884. Two years later, when Cort learned that his daughter had died and left a child, he was uninterested. Mattie Silks, however, adopted the girl and placed her in a good foster home, paying for her room and board.

Silks gave her husband money to gamble and bought him a horse ranch in Wray, Colorado. There are some reports that her adopted daughter also came and spent some time at the ranch.

On at least one occasion, Mattie Silks had occasion to use her pistols. One night in 1891, in a local rooming house, Mattie found Thompson with another woman, Lillie Dab. Silks pulled out her pistol and fired. She didn't hit anyone, although some versions of the tale report that the bullet Mattie fired clipped off one of Lillie's curls. The frightened woman left and an angry Thompson beat up Mattie.

Because of this major blow up, Mattie filed for divorce and kicked Cort out. She couldn't seem to stay angry at him though, and when he came back begging forgiveness, she relented and didn't go through with the divorce.

It was not unusual for a madam to take her girls on a summer "vacation." Perhaps they would go to a mining camp where the madam would set up tents and run her business for a few weeks before returning to the city. Mattie and Cort Thompson made an extended trip to Alaska for pleasure and for business. She took along a few of her girls and opened a house in Dawson, Alaska. After a time, they returned to Denver.

Cort Thompson was at the ranch in Wray when he became very ill. Silks rushed to the ranch to nurse him, but he died before she arrived. Cort died in 1900 when Mattie was only fifty-four years old. She arranged and paid for a very expensive funeral for him and bought the adjoining plot in the cemetery for herself.

Toward the end of 1900, there was an attempt to rein in the red light district of Denver. The Denver City Council passed an ordinance requiring that all prostitutes wear yellow ribbons on their clothing to denote their profession. This supposedly would allow other women to avoid these courtesans. The very next day, the ladies of the parlor houses, led by Mattie Silks and Jennie Rogers, marched as a group down Fifteenth Street dressed in shoes, dresses, hats, and ribbons completely in yellow. The city ordinance faded away.

Mattie Silks continued to run her business in Denver. When Jennie Rogers died, Silks bought the House of Mirrors from the Rogers estate. She ran it for three years, selling it in 1919. After that, the House of Mirrors was used for a time as a Buddhist temple.

Mattie Silks then took up with Handsome Jack Ready, a man several years younger than she. He was described as "a big fellow with sandy red hair and two gold front teeth with a diamond set in the center." Jack Ready had worked for a time at the Wray ranch as a foreman. Mattie employed him as a bouncer and financial advisor for her parlor house. Then they began living together. They threw expensive and wild parties and traveled a good deal. Jack helped her spend her money. In 1923, at the age of seventy-seven, Mattie Silks married Handsome Jack Ready.

Mattie and her new husband moved into a house on Laurence Street where they lived until her death in 1929. At that point, although she'd made lots of money during her lifetime, she and her men had spent most of it. Mattie Silks's estate was small and it was divided between her adopted granddaughter and her husband. Silks was buried in the cemetery plot she had bought right next to Cort Thompson.

Shrewd businesswomen who sometimes acted like jerks, Jennie Rogers and Mattie Silks used cons, pistols, and bribes to survive as Denver madams.

SOURCES

Armitage, Susan, and Elizabeth Jameson. *The Women's West.* Norman, OK: University of Oklahoma Press, 1987. Discusses the myths and realities of women who homesteaded or engaged in various occupations in the West.

Butler, Anne M. *Daughters of Joy, Sisters of Misery: Prostitutes in the American West, 1865-90.* Chicago: University of Illinois Press, 1985. Shares some of the poverty and misery that made up much of the life of prostitutes.

Couch, Jacqualine Grannell. *Those Golden Girls of Market Street: An Historical Glimpse.* Fort Collins, CO: Old Army Press, 1974. This is a brief discussion of four of Denver's famous madams.

Enss, Chris. *Pistol Packin' Madams: True Stories of Notorious Women of the Old West.* Guilford, CT: Globe Pequot Press, 2006.

MacKell, Jan. *Brothels, Bordellos, and Bad Girls: Prostitution in Colorado 1860–1930.* Albuquerque, NM: University of New Mexico Press, 2004. A general history of prostitution in Colorado mining camps and cities.

Pryor, Alton. *Bawdy House Girls: A Look at the Brothels of the Old West.* Roseville, CA: Sagebrush Publishing, 2006. Contains short profiles of some well known prostitutes and some discussion of both the lures and desperation of their lives.

Rutter, Michael. *Upstairs Girls: Prostitution in the American West.* Helena, MT: Farcountry Press, 2005.

Seagraves, Anne. *Soiled Doves: Prostitution in the Early West.* Hayden, ID: Wesanne Publications, 1994.

Wommack, Lindar. *Our Ladies of the Tenderloin: Colorado's Legends in Lace.* Caldwell, ID: Caxton Press, 2005. A well researched book on prostitution in the nineteenth century in Colorado.

Wood, Richard E. *Here Lies Colorado: Fascinating Figures in Colorado History.* Helena, MT: Farcountry Press, 2005.

CHAPTER 13

Adjutant General John Chase and Lieutenant Karl Linderfeldt

THE LUDLOW MASSACRE

*O**n April 20, 1914, Ludlow, Colorado, was the scene of a bloody fight for coal miners' rights. The striking miners and their families had been thrown out of their company houses and were living in tent cities. Colorado Governor Elias Ammons called in the militia led by Adjutant General John Chase. Although the militia was to keep the peace and be impartial, it soon become apparent that many members of the militia were in fact being paid by the mine owners to try to break the strike.*

Early in the morning on April 20, mine guards and state militia led by Lieutenant Karl Linderfeldt fired guns into the tent city and rode through on horseback. Using brooms dipped in kerosene as torches, they set fire to the tent city. Some of the miners and their family members were shot, some burned, and others suffocated in dugout shelters beneath the tents. The strike was broken. In their abuse of power and attacks on defenseless miners and their families, both General Chase and Lieutenant Linderfeldt proved themselves to be unforgivable jerks.

The dreaded Death Mobile, an armored car with a mounted machine gun, had made several trips into the tent city of miners at Ludlow, Colorado. When it appeared, the striking miners knew to keep out of the way, and the women and children in the tents scurried down into pits dug beneath their houses. Several times guards and soldiers marched through the tent city, scattering the miners' possessions and stealing whatever took their fancy while searching for guns. But on this day the soldiers rode through the

General John Chase (center, in light uniform)
COURTESY COLORADO HISTORICAL SOCIETY

city bearing torches and setting fire to the tents, as well as spraying bullets through the air. Mine owners had declared war on the strikers. This was the Ludlow Massacre.

In the early 1900s the fatality rate of Colorado miners was double that of anywhere else in the world. Coal miners were desperate for major improvements in their working conditions. In most mines, there was no medical assistance available when a worker was injured. Miners were forced to work more than an eight-hour day. They were paid only for the number of tons of coal they dug, not for time spent in putting up timbers or laying tracks. They felt cheated by the weigh-man, whom they accused of underrecording the weight of the coal, which determined their wages. Those who complained were fired. The workers had no union and no one to represent them who had bargaining power with the mine owners.

In many of the coal mining towns, miners had to live in fenced camps that were patrolled by armed guards. In these places where families were permitted to live with the miners, the miners had to purchase all their food and other supplies within their tent city. Rather than being paid in money, the miners were paid in "script" which could only be used in a company store. When ill, they were seen by a company doctor. When they died, many were buried in a plot purchased in a company-owned cemetery.

Union organizers of the United Mine Workers of America tried to recruit new members from among the coal miners who had many legitimate grievances. One of the men's biggest complaints was that their wages were determined by the weight of their carloads of coal. The miners said they were often cheated on the scales by as much as four hundred to eight hundred pounds because the weigh-in man was not honest. The miners wanted to elect the man for this position rather than have him appointed by the mine owners.

When it appeared that the United Mine Workers union was succeeding in getting enough members to be in a position to make demands, union organizers and members were fired. Sometimes these men were threatened, beaten, taken across state lines, and warned never to return. In their place, cheap foreign laborers were hired.

Most workers in northern Colorado were born in the United States and spoke English. In southern Colorado coal fields, many nationalities were represented, including men from Greece, Croatia, Italy, Austria, Serbia, Germany, Romania, Bulgaria, Hungary, Russia, and Poland. Often these newly hired men did not speak English, had no mine experience, and were therefore prone to accidents.

In 1913, the miners drew up a list of seven demands: recognition of a union; a pay raise; an eight-hour work day; pay for dead work (timbering, laying rail, etc.); a weigh-in man elected by the miners; the right to trade in a store of their choice, select their own boarding places, and choose their own doctor; the enforcement of Colorado mining laws; and the elimination of camp mine guards.

Governor Elias Milton Ammons did not want trouble in the mines. He encouraged mine operators of the big three (Colorado Fuel and Iron Company, Rocky Mountain Fuel, and Victor-American Fuel) to meet with the United Mine Workers union officials. The governor sent the state labor commissioner to organize a conference to be held on August 17, 1913.

Gerald Lippiatt came to Trinidad to participate in this conference with the mine owners as a representative of northern Colorado mine workers. He got in a quarrel with two agents from the Baldwin-Felts Agency who had been hired by the mine owners as strike breakers. Lippiatt was shot dead in the street, and this ruined any chance for friendly discussions between mine owners and union officials. The mine owners ignored the grievances and demands of the workers. Union members were furious, and a strike was called on September 23, 1913.

When the miners went on strike, they and their families were promptly evicted from company houses. Using union funds, land east of the Ludlow coal camps was rented. The union put up tent colonies for the use of striking miners and their families. Most of these tent homes had wooden floors and wooden walls. There was a cook stove in the middle of the tent and posts to hold up a tent roof. Most of the tent cities included a large tent that could be used as a meeting hall or for school classes. The striking miners began moving into the tent cities located at Walsenburg, Rugby, Aguilar, Forbes, Suffield, Sopris, Starkville, and Ludlow. The largest of these tent cities was at Ludlow, which was designed to hold 1,200 residents.

The workers hoped that the mine owners would quickly see that this time the coal miners were serious about staying out on strike and would be forced to meet the workers' demands. Instead, the mine owners increased the guards around their property, hired more Baldwin-Felts detectives, and bought up a large supply of rifles and ammunition. The Baldwin-Felts agents in the past had been used to track down criminals and to investigate train robberies, but at this time and place, they were being used to break strikes.

Governor Elias Ammons finally got representatives of the mine owners and striking miners together to negotiate, and many of the miners' demands were met. But the mine owners would not agree that the miners could have union representation, so when it came to a vote, the miners rejected the agreement.

The Colorado Fuel and Iron Company, the largest coal mining operation in the state of Colorado, had a special armored car built. It had bulletproof sides and a machine gun mounted on the back. It quickly earned the nickname of the Death Mobile. Gunmen sometimes took the Death Mobile and drove near the tent cities, spraying bullets at random into the tents. Because of this, some miners dug pits under their tents. In time of danger, their families could hide there to be safe from bullets.

On October 17, 1913, the Baldwin-Felts detectives in the Death Mobile visited and fired on the tents at the Forbes colony. One striker was killed and two children were injured. Governor Ammons decided he needed to take a firsthand look at what was happening. He left Denver for Trinidad on October 21 and checked into the Cardenas Hotel. Famous activist Mother Jones led a demonstration outside the hotel on the afternoon he arrived. The lobby of the hotel quickly filled with union officials and business leaders. Among these people hoping to talk to the governor was Lieutenant Karl Linderfeldt. Ammons talked with as many people as he could and went on several visits to the mines. While Governor Ammons was there, it was decided that Lieutenant Linderfeldt would command the deputies at Ludlow.

Fearing violence on both sides, on October 28, 1913, Governor Ammons committed to call out the National Guard of Colorado. These men would be charged with being impartial, and it was stated that no company guards would be enlisted in the militia. In the days and weeks that followed, however, the members of the state militia were replaced by guards and gunmen hired by the mine owners. Some of the men who were enlisted into the Guard were being paid by both the mine owners and as Guardsmen.

On November 1, 1913, General John Chase and his 931 men arrived and made camps at Trinidad and Walsenburg. The governor's orders were to protect nonstriking men who were not on strike and who wanted to continue to work in the mines, to keep strikebreakers out, and to disarm unauthorized persons. At this point many of the miners had weapons, and they were not willing to give them up.

During these tense times, a nonstriking worker was threatened and bullied one evening by armed miners who were on strike. The man escaped and called for an army escort home. A car came for him, but the striking miners ambushed the car, killing the driver and three guards. The nonstriking miner got away.

Such a violent incident was exactly what General Chase needed to establish his authority. Eight miners were immediately arrested for the shooting. The district attorney of Las Animas County released four of these miners due to lack of evidence. General Chase ordered these four men locked up again, claiming that he had supreme power under martial law. The district attorney insisted that martial law had not been declared, and he telegraphed the governor. The governor bowed to the advice of General Chase, who set up a military tribunal. On November 15, General Chase notified District Attorney Hendricks that all persons arrested as military prisoners would be judged by a tribunal of seven men whom he had appointed to be judges. (One of these supposedly impartial judges was a mine owner's lawyer.)

The winter of 1913–14 was especially hard on the coal miners in their tent cities. United Mine Workers records, confirmed by the *Rocky Mountain News*, indicated that 11,132 of Colorado's 13,980 coal miners were on strike. Food was scarce. Winter storms often blew tents down in the miners' tent cities.

Men in the militia suffered, too. They also were living in tents during the cold weather. Sometimes their pay was held back. While this did not affect officers such as General Chase and Lieutenant

Linderfeldt, many of the troopers were in poor shape. Their boots were worn through and their uniforms were ragged. They didn't have money to send home to their families.

Another unhappy event helped brand the striking miners as violent. The Baldwin-Felts detective, George Belcher, who had shot and killed Gerald Lippiatt in the street back in August, was generally hated by the miners. Fearing for his life, he always wore a steel vest. A gunman, believed to have been hired by the miners, shot Belcher in the head and killed him on November 20. A man named Zancanelli was arrested and confessed.

General Chase and his men continued to harass the union miners and organizers. Chase jailed forty-three miners on various charges ranging from murder to buying guns with the intent of overthrowing society. These men were denied the right to see lawyers, make appeals, or receive visitors. The general said these rights had been suspended during martial law. As a result, a huge march in mid-December demanded the ouster of the governor and the recall of General Chase. The governor insisted that to recall the general, he needed proof that the officers were siding with the coal mine owners.

On December 30, Lieutenant Linderfeldt and some of his men went on horseback to pull a car out of a snow bank. Under the snow was barbed wire. One horse tripped and the rider was injured. Lieutenant Linderfeldt insisted that the barbed wire was a trap set for his men by some miners.

Lieutenant Linderfeldt had quickly become one of the most hated figures in the strike area. Born into a Scandinavian family in 1876 in Janesville, Wisconsin, he attended Beloit College for a time and then headed west to try his luck as a gold miner. He joined the Rough Riders to fight in Cuba, but was ill and missed most of the action. Then he went to the Philippines to serve in the American force charged with putting down nationalist insurgents.

Perhaps it was during his service in the Philippines in 1899 and 1900 that he acquired the attitude that made him so feared and hated in the Colorado coalfields. He had participated in the destruction and burning of stores and homes, actions that had become unofficial policy of the soldiers in that war. He also served as a mercenary during a 1910 revolution in Mexico and narrowly missed being court-martialed for looting in Juarez.

After he returned to the United States, Linderfeldt worked as a company guard at Cripple Creek. He wore the uniform of the state militia when he joined General Chase and assisted in crushing the Western Federation strike.

This violent background in dealing with various insurrections no doubt guided Linderfeldt in his dealings with the striking Colorado coal miners. Wanting to act quickly to punish those he thought had set the barbed wire trap for his men, he arrested several suspects, including Louis Tikas, who denied having any knowledge of the barbed wire. Lieutenant Linderfeldt told him he would file charges in the morning.

Tikas had attended the University of Athens and was highly regarded by Colorado coal miners. He often served as a translator for the Greek workers with limited English. Observers feared a bloody uprising if any harm came to Tikas. Perhaps because of Tikas's standing in the community, General Chase released Tikas that night.

The next morning, General Chase ordered his militia to search Ludlow for arms. Linderfeldt and his men surrounded the area on horseback, while other militia men went through the tents. The militia did find some rifles, but they also helped themselves to watches, money, knives, and anything else of value.

On January 4, 1914, spirits rose briefly when a famous labor organizer appeared in Trinidad. It was Mary Harris Jones, or Mother Jones. At this time she was near eighty years old. She had a remarkable history across the country of aiding striking miners. General Chase had his men arrest her at the station and put her on the next train to Denver. She was warned that if she came back to Trinidad, she would be arrested. But come back she did on January 11. General Chase himself arrested her this time and took her to the San Rafael Hospital, where she was guarded under military surveillance.

Ten days later, the women and children from the tent cities staged a parade in Trinidad, demanding the release of Mother Jones. Adjutant General Chase confronted the marchers. Somehow in the crowd, confusion, and excitement, the general fell from his horse. Those in the parade had a good laugh and mocked him. The angry general remounted and like a true jerk ordered his men to "ride down the women." With bared sabers, the men rode through the women and children and injured a number of them.

On March 10 a strikebreaker was killed by a train. The train crew said he might have wandered onto the tracks in a drunken state. General Chase insisted that strikers had beaten the man and laid him across the tracks. In retaliation, the general ordered his men to go to the tent city of Forbes, to which he said his bloodhounds had followed a scent, and to tear down their tents.

After ten weeks of detention, Mother Jones was released and told not to come back to southern Colorado. Of course she returned, and the general locked her up again, this time in the basement of the Walsenburg courthouse.

Lieutenant Linderfeldt swore in as militia a local company of men, called Troop A, who were largely mine guards and bosses and vigilantes. These men had no military training and did not even have uniforms. Although it had been made clear from the beginning that such men should not be in the militia, which was supposed to be an unbiased group, General Chase accepted them.

The strike continued for weeks and then months. On Monday, April 20, 1914, the firing on the tent city of Ludlow began. A stream of bullets riddled the tents. Chaos enveloped the camp. At least one man ran down the railroad tracks toward Trinidad to get help. One woman, Mary Thomas, wife of a Welsh miner, gathered many women and children and hurried them to a spot near the railway tracks where they were safe. Led by Lieutenant Linderfeldt, soldiers on horseback rode through the camp. They dipped brooms in kerosene to make torches and then ignited as many of the tents as they could. Frightened women and children ran ahead of the horsemen, fleeing burning tents, and were shot as they ran.

The Greek leader of the Ludlow Camp, Louis Tikas, who had already had run-ins with Lieutenant Linderfeldt, was captured by the militia soon after the tents were fired. Tikas was brought before Lieutenant Linderfeldt. The lieutenant bashed Tikas's head with his rifle, and when Tikas turned and tried to move away, he was shot three times in the back. His body was left lying where it fell so that other miners and their families would see it as they were escorted out of camp. Completely out of control, the men looted anything of value in the camp as they went.

Many of the women and children retreated to an arroyo, where they were protected from bullets. From there, they made their way east toward a wooded area. Miners from Trinidad, who came to Ludlow when they learned what had happened, put up tents to shelter these women and children. Two days would pass before the Red Cross, undertakers, and reporters were allowed to enter the camp.

As is the case with all such events, the exact number of dead was disputed. It is certain that at least four men, two women, and eleven children died. Some were shot, some burned, and one group that had taken shelter in the dugout under a tent suffocated. That spot was given the name "The Black Hole of Ludlow." A huge wooden cross made of burnt mine timbers was erected there in their memory and was eventually replaced by a permanent memorial.

The bodies of those who died at Ludlow were taken to a mortuary in Trinidad. Strangely enough, that night the mortuary caught fire, and the bodies of the mine victims had to be taken out into the street to preserve them. The cause of the mortuary fire was never discovered. When the funerals for the Ludlow victims were held, hundreds of mourners paraded, without violence of any kind.

When the events at Ludlow made national news, the mine owners were quick to try to shift the blame on the miners, insisting that the workers started the fight there, and that the fire in the tents was the result of an overturned stove. They said all the reports of the so-called "massacre" were wildly distorted.

Furious miners began taking revenge. Dozens of mine installations in the surrounding area were dynamited and burned, costing mine operators thousands of dollars. Many times at these sites, the cry of "Remember Ludlow" was heard. Governor Elias Ammons was finally forced to call in federal troops.

The first federal troops, under the command of Major McClure, arrived in Denver on April 29, and promptly moved to Trinidad. They were welcomed by the miners because they had been ordered to be absolutely neutral in the dispute.

President Woodrow Wilson established a United States Commission of Industrial Regulation to investigate the Ludlow incident. In the report, the commission wrote, "The State of Colorado through its military arm was rendered helpless to maintain law and order because that military arm acted, not as an agent of the commonwealth, but as an agent of one of the parties in interest, as an agent, that is, of the coal operators as against the strikers."

A military court convened in Golden in May 1914 and was charged with reporting its findings to Governor Ammons. Some felt that accusations against the miners and their families at Ludlow were brought before a military court to avoid having the officers risk a trial in civilian courts. The court was to consider whether the military was responsible for setting fire to the tents. The charges against Lieutenant Karl Linderfeldt also included: responsibility for exacerbating tensions between strikers and soldiers; murder of women and children; larceny; firing machine guns into the colony causing the death of Frank Snyder; and assault with a deadly weapon on Tikas.

Because of the many additional charges against Lieutenant Linderfeldt, he was tried separately from the other men. Most of the accused were acquitted in separate trials taking no longer than half a day each. Before Linderfeldt testified, four sentries were suddenly placed around the grounds to halt all comers who could not explain why they wanted to attend the meeting. These sentries had not been in place before Linderfeldt's trial. At his trial, Lieutenant Linderfelt testified that he had refrained from firing at the striking miners and that during heavy fire he rushed into the tent colony, dropped his rifle, and carried out children in his arms. His testimony of the events at Ludlow was entered into the record without question or cross-examination. The *Denver Post* ran a front page article based on his testimony on May 16 that said, "Lieutenant Linderfeldt hero at Ludlow if what he tells court martial is the truth."

Other officers did not see Lieutenant Linderfeldt as a hero. Captain Philip Van Cise had observed how Linderfeldt seemed to enjoy generally annoying the miners at every opportunity. Van Cise described Linderfeldt as a "typical soldier of fortune," and "the worst man that could have been put in command of troops charged with preserving the peace."

Lieutenant Linderfeldt did testify that he hit Louis Tikas over the head with his Springfield rifle, shattering the rifle stock. That assault was the only charge that was eventually sustained against him. The judges attached no criminality to this charge, but he was reduced in rank.

The results of the military trial were quite different from the 1914 report from the Colorado State Federation of Labor, "Militarism in Colorado: Report of the Committee Appointed at the Suggestion of the Governor of Colorado to Investigate the Conduct of the Colorado National Guard during the Coal Strike of 1913–1914." That report singled out Linderfeldt to be condemned. It says, "He is wholly an unfit man to bear arms and command men, as he has no control over himself."

No sooner was the military trial ended than 162 striking miners were indicted. Most of these were transferred from military into civil custody. Among those charged was John Lawson, a United Mine Workers leader, accused of murdering a mine guard named John Nimmo. Two mine guards who were with Nimmo when he was shot testified that John Lawson was not there and that Nimmo in fact had been killed by friendly fire. Lawson's trial took less than two weeks, and he was convicted of first-degree murder. His attorney appealed, and requested a new trial, Lawson was released on bail.

Some members of the press were surprised that in closed court, militiamen were acquitted and they thought that the verdict for John Lawson was "amazing." While Lawson's lawyer was tied up in court, Judge Granby Hillyer ordered Lawson before him and in one of his final acts on the bench denied Lawson's petition for a new trial and sentenced Lawson to life in prison. Lawson's attorney petitioned the Colorado Supreme Court and they released Lawson on bond. Two years later, the Colorado Supreme Court overturned all the convictions against the strikers including John Lawson.

The United Mine Workers bought forty acres of land around the Black Hole at Ludlow, and on April 20, 1917, dedicated that land in a ceremony that brought thousands of miners to the spot. Those who came wore red bandanas as a symbol of the miners and carried American flags, including the flag that had flown over Ludlow.

It was hoped that the events at Ludlow, and the ceremony held at the Black Hole, would bring about a quick improvement of working conditions for miners. This was not to come for many years. In fact, a week after the Ludlow memorial ceremony, there was an explosion in a mine just a few miles from the monument. The Hastings Mine was known for its dangerous gases and had suffered an explosion back in 1912 that took the lives of a dozen men. This time, 121 men died in the 1917 Hastings Mine explosion.

And what happened to Lieutenant Linderfeldt who acted like a bloodthirsty jerk at Ludlow? He was demoted but went on to serve in the army during World War I. Afterwards he moved to Oklahoma and applied for a military pension. Eventually, he moved to Los Angeles, and after his death in 1958, he was buried in the national cemetery for veterans.

Sources

Johnson, Marilynn S. *Violence in the West*. Boston, MA: Bedford/ St. Martins, 2009.

Laughlin, Rosemary. *The Ludlow Massacre of 1912–14*. Greensboro, NC: Morgan Reynolds Publishing, 2006.

Martelle, Scott. *Blood Passion: The Ludlow Massacre and Class War of the American West*. New Brunswick, NJ: The Rutgers University Press, 2007.

Papanikolas, Zeese. *Buried Unsung: Louis Tikas and the Ludlow Massacre*. Lincoln, NE: University of Nebraska Press, 1982.

Sampson, Joanna. *"Remember Ludlow!"* Denver, CO: Colorado Historical Society, 1999.

Smith, Phyllis. *Once A Coal Miner. The Story of Colorado's Northern Coal Field*. Boulder, CO: Pruett Publishing, 1989.

Stein, Leon, and Philip Taft, eds. *Massacre at Ludlow: Four Reports*. New York: Arno Press, 1971.

Tarasenko, Kathryn. *The Media on the Ludlow Massacre: Objective Witness or Tool of Government and Big Business?* Greeley, CO: University of Northern Colorado Thesis, College of Arts & Sciences, Department of Journalism and Mass Communication, May 1996.

Winford, Jessica L. *An Analysis of Ivy Lee's Handling of the Ludlow Massacre: An Application of Grunig's Models of Public Relations*. Greeley, CO: University of Northern Colorado, College of Arts & Sciences, Department of Journalism and Mass Communication, 2003.

CHAPTER 14

Benjamin Franklin Stapleton

DURING THE REIGN OF THE KKK

*W*hen someone aims at being elected mayor of a large city like Denver, Colorado, the candidate must appeal to many con- stituents to win. Ben Stapleton was well aware of this. During the first half of the 1920s in Denver, the Ku Klux Klan wielded tre- mendous political power. Ben Stapleton made use of that power. The record book of the Denver Ku Klux Klan shows Stapleton as member number 1128. He even addressed the Klan at large rallies. Yet in his run for mayor, Stapleton did not mention any Klan con- nections. In fact he stated during his campaign that "true Ameri- canism needs no masks or disguise." In deceiving the public about his Klan connections even while accepting the Klan's help to gain office and doing their bidding as mayor of Denver, Ben Stapleton revealed himself to be a bona fide jerk.

It was 1924 and the United Negroes Protective Association in Den- ver made an application. They wanted to build a home for black senior citizens at 1117 30th Street. Mayor Ben Stapleton's admin- istration promptly vetoed this effort saying it would be a hazard to public health. That October, the case reached the Colorado Supreme Court, which overrode the city ruling. The court found in favor of the Protective Association and gave them the right to pro- ceed with their project. Why would a home for seniors be vetoed by Mayor Stapleton's administration? This was a small but striking example of the power the Colorado Ku Klux Klan wielded during Stapleton's first two terms of office. The Klan, while being pro– law-and-order, and pro-citizenship, was definitely anti-foreigner, anti-Jew, anti-Catholic, and anti–African American. Stapleton's appointments to countless positions on boards and commissions

Benjamin F. Stapleton (right)
COURTESY COLORADO HISTORICAL SOCIETY

and in city government supported the venomous prejudice of the KKK.

During the spring of 1923, there was considerable talk about who would be elected mayor. It was supposed to be a nonpartisan race, but the two major parties were clearly vying for power. The field of candidates was wide open, with neither the Democrats nor the Republicans offering a single candidate who looked like a winner. After World War I, the city of Denver had seemed to lack leadership and drifted along. There was a high crime rate and general dissatisfaction with how the city was being run. The incumbent, Mayor Bailey, was heartily disliked by many sections of the community. It was the perfect time for Benjamin Franklin Stapleton to make his big political move.

Ben Stapleton was born on November 12, 1869 in Paintsville, Kentucky. He lived on a farm and went to school in Kentucky until he moved with his family to Howard Lake, Minnesota. After the family moved again to Ohio, Stapleton earned a degree from National Normal University in Lebanon, Ohio, and began working as a school principal in Waverly, Minnesota.

Stapleton then did course work in 1894 at National Normal Law School. Apparently he did not actually earn a law degree nor take any standard examinations but, on the basis of character letters, was admitted to the bar in Marysville, Kentucky. On February 14, 1895, Stapleton got permission to practice law in Colorado—again without taking any examinations, but purely on the basis that he had already been admitted to the Kentucky Bar Association.

Stapleton opened a law office in Denver in 1896 but handled very few cases. Perhaps it was because he had such a small practice that he enlisted in the First Colorado Regiment and went to fight in the Spanish-American War. He served as a quartermaster sergeant and was stationed in the Philippines for a year.

After his discharge, Stapleton did not go back to his law practice but went to work in the county clerk's office. He helped organize a veteran's group called the Colorado Society of the Army of the Philippines that eventually merged with the Veterans of Foreign Wars. Stapleton served a couple terms as president of this group.

Next he moved from the county clerk's office to a post in the treasurer's office. Then he was elected to serve as one of the three justices of the peace for the city and county of Denver. Stapleton dealt with criminal matters as a police magistrate. In 1910 Mayor Speer appointed Stapleton to a four-year term as the judge of the police court. Stapleton did not drink or smoke and was known to come down hard on anything he regarded as a lapse of morality. He once fined a woman for showing eight inches of her leg above the ankle when stepping onto a streetcar. At the same time that he built up his image as a strong, law-and-order morals man, like a good politician he seemed able to ignore prostitution and gambling spots that had ties to Mayor Speer.

When a new mayor, Henry Arnold, was elected in June 1912, he asked for Stapleton's resignation so that he might appoint one of his own supporters. Stapleton refused to step down. The new mayor then tried to remove Stapleton on the basis of six accusations of misconduct. The misconduct included two accusations that Stapleton had gone from precinct to precinct in a city car trying to line up votes for Mayor Speer, that he had suspended a fine against a vagrant, that he had appointed a non-Denver resident as bailiff of the court, that he had allowed two clerks to engage in Democratic electioneering, and that he had created a court atmosphere that was hostile to attorneys.

The city council, with Mayor Arnold presiding, met to consider these charges. Henry Lindsey, Speers's longtime city attorney, defended Stapleton and challenged whether the proceedings were even legal. Mayor Arnold, however, overruled all of Lindsey's objections to the proceedings. Stapleton responded to the charges against him, insisting that he was an impartial judge and that although he had not supported Arnold for mayor, he would not resign his position.

After two days of testimony, the board of aldermen gathered and ruled that Stapleton was not fit for office. The board of supervisors, however, felt that the city's case against Stapleton had not been convincing. Since they had the final authority, they tabled the removal petition and did not act upon it. Stapleton remained police judge. This was the first of many times that Stapleton fought tenaciously to hold on to a position.

In the 1913 election, when the people held a popular vote to elect the commissioner of social welfare, Stapleton came in fourth in a field of twenty-nine candidates. He was becoming a strong candidate in the Democratic Party. When the new commission met on June 2, they selected Stapleton as one of the two justices of the peace. Proving himself to be a bitter enemy to the very end, Mayor Arnold promptly fired Stapleton from his new appointment. When Mayor Arnold officially left office on June 7, however, Stapleton resumed his position as police judge/justice of the peace.

On February 25, 1915, Stapleton was rewarded for his faithful service to the Democratic Party with an appointment by

President Woodrow Wilson to postmaster of Denver. That same day, Stapleton suffered a great personal loss when his wife died at age thirty-nine. Two years later, Stapleton married Mabel Freeland, a talented music teacher. Over the next few years, the couple had a son and a daughter. Stapleton supported President Wilson throughout World War I and was active as a Veteran's of Foreign Wars representative to the Colorado Patriotic League.

On December 1, 1921, Stapleton resigned as Denver postmaster to work for Western Oil Fields. There, most of his colleagues were Republicans. When Stapleton decided to run for mayor in 1923, he hoped that his nonpartisan campaign would be supported by Republican financiers as well as Democrats, and promised he would have a nonpartisan administration. He committed himself to providing a "clean and efficient" administration where "business and not politics" would be the rule. There were rumors at this time that Stapleton had ties to the Ku Klux Klan. Although he never spoke out directly against the KKK, he produced a piece of widely circulated campaign literature pledging that "Any attempt to stir up racial prejudices or religious intolerance is contrary to our constitution and is therefore un-American."

As the voting day approached, there was real uncertainty as to which of the many candidates might win. It snowed on election day, and city offices closed. Some thought the incumbent mayor unnecessarily closed offices so that municipal employees could spend that day helping to re-elect their boss. At that time, Denver citizens were given the chance to vote for a first, second, and third choice among the candidates. It was the combination of these votes that determined which candidate won. When the results came in, Stapleton was the narrow winner in a field of eight candidates. Although this was supposed to have been a nonpartisan election, it was considered a major Democratic Party victory. At his victory dinner, Stapleton promised a cost-efficient government.

Stapleton had a simple swearing in ceremony, and the city council generally supported him. At first there appeared to be no one at city hall who was a special champion of Ku Klux

Klan causes. But it did not take long before the influence of the KKK was felt. South Denver councilman, Harry Risley, joined the Klan. Rice Means, a powerful Klansman, was appointed by Stapleton to two posts: city attorney and manager of safety. In turn, Means appointed Charles Lewis, another Klansman, to be secretary of the department of safety. Between them, Means and Lewis appointed Klansmen to powerful positions in the police department, especially to key positions involving gambling, rum-running, and prostitution.

Rice Means became Ben Stapleton's chief advisor. At the same time, the Colorado branch of the Ku Klux Klan presided over by John Galen Locke was recognized as the "Realm of Colorado" and became an important part of the national Klan movement. At a big celebration marking the first anniversary of the Colorado Klan on May 13, 1923, speakers included City Attorney Rice Means, Chief of Police William Candlish, and Judge Clarence Morley, who later that year would be elected governor. Thanks to Stapleton's appointments, the KKK in Colorado had a firm grip on Denver and Colorado politics.

Becoming more overt in their actions, the Colorado Klan received permission to use the Denver Auditorium for a big Klan speech and rally. George C. Minor, a national lecturer and leader in the Klan from Texas, was scheduled to be the featured speaker. When people objected to the rally, Stapleton first professed not to have known about it, then he began meeting with various groups to discuss the matter. Governor William Sweet was among those who sent a telegraph to Mayor Stapleton, asking him to stop the meeting and pointing out that "the Ku Klux Klan is neither needed nor wanted in Colorado."

Bowing to public sentiment, Commissioner Ormsley on the morning of the lecture, June 27, denied the KKK permission to use the hall. At noon Mayor Stapleton overrode the commissioner's order. To appease angry citizens, Stapleton insisted, however, that the people who attended the speech could not wear robes or burn crosses. The auditorium opened at eight o'clock that evening to crowds of both Klansmen and the curious. Four thousand people came to hear Minor speak.

On stage Minor said that he was a law abiding citizen and that if anyone in the auditorium objected to his talking, he would cancel his speech. After a moment's silence, a few men stood. Minor said since there was dissention, he would cancel the meeting. With that he left the stage and within fifteen minutes the auditorium was empty.

Much talk resulted from the cancellation of the speech. Some took the opportunity to denounce the Klan; others sought membership thinking this was a huge and powerful group with the ability to advance their careers. From this time forward, the liberals who had helped elect Stapleton to office found it harder to gain access to him, while John Galen Locke, grand dragon of the Colorado Klan, became a common figure at city hall.

With Klansmen in key posts in the police department, efforts were made to take over power in the fire department. To a large extent this failed because the current fire chief, John F. Healy, held a civil service position with seniority and qualifications and could not easily be dismissed. Locke and other Klansmen tried to change this provision of the law knowing that they could then persuade Mayor Stapleton to appoint a Klansman as fire chief and thereby rid the fire departments of Catholics. The Klan was unsuccessful in its efforts largely because insurance industries supported Chief Healy and his crews that had kept losses and insurance rates low. Healy remained fire chief until his death.

Stapleton, however, continued to appoint Klansmen as police judges and constables. Klan members were also appointed to the city's civil service commission. When Rice Means was elected to the U.S. Senate, Mayor Stapleton appointed Henry F. May to be Denver city attorney. May had previously served as a Klan attorney.

Increasingly, John Galen Locke, grand dragon of the KKK, was making decisions for Mayor Stapleton. When Stapleton seemed about to step out of line and exert his own influence, the Klan threatened to recall him. Such threats put Stapleton back in line, and he would make another Klan-approved appointment. Such was the case when he appointed William Candlish as chief of police.

Candlish proved to be a big mistake. He designed a fancy uniform for himself that earned him the nickname "Gold Braid Bill." He also spent a lot of time across the street from city hall at a soft drink parlor, which earned him another nickname, "Coca-Cola Candlish," or "Koka-Kola Kandlish," because of his ties with the KKK. Candlish openly recruited Klansmen to the police force, pressured officers to join the Klan, and assigned dangerous beats and midnight shifts to those who didn't follow him.

Crime was on the increase in the city. At one point, the grand dragon offered the use of 5,000 Klansmen volunteers to assist the police in fighting crime. Mayor Stapleton actually accepted this offer, but before the volunteers were called in to work, the press put the matter on the front pages. Newspapers were highly critical of the mayor for suggesting turning law enforcement over to a vigilante group. In response to this public outcry, the volunteers were never used.

Because of the obvious Klan pressure on Stapleton, and especially after the appointment of Candlish as chief of police, a petition was started in February 1924 to recall the mayor. Although the petition listed six areas in which Stapleton had supposedly failed the city, it carefully did not directly mention his connection with the Ku Klux Klan for fear of repercussions. Petitioners had ninety days to collect 17,761 signatures. At first many people were reluctant to sign, but when it came out that Stapleton actually was a member of the Klan, signatures picked up dramatically. On March 29, 1924, the recall petition was submitted with 26,362 signatures.

At first, the city clerk and recorder, William Lail, refused to accept the petition on a Saturday, saying that that office was closed for the weekend. When it was pointed out that it was just before noon and the office was open on Saturdays until 1:00 p.m., Lail reluctantly accepted the petition. Stapleton and his supporters met over the weekend, trying to find a way to derail the recall. On Tuesday, city clerk William Lail rejected the recall petition using a variety of legal grounds. The Colorado Supreme Court then took jurisdiction. The court upheld the legality of the petition on May 9, and Lail was told to process the signatures.

In the meantime, Mayor Stapleton and his supporters were active. Lail gave them access to the petitions, and all signatures and addresses on the petition were copied onto cards. As Mayor Stapleton used these cards to check on the validity of the signers, numerous errors were found. Spelling of names was incorrect. People did not live at their listed address. Some signatures were declared forgeries; some belonged to aliens; some were duplicates; some were from underage people; some came from people who now admitted they'd been offered bribes to sign. After this investigation, the mayor said that 16,410 of the petitioners' names were bogus.

About one thousand citizens whose signatures had been challenged for one reason or another were ordered to report to the courthouse, which was the headquarters of the elections committee. There was such a crowd that many could not get in the building and had to wait outside. Most were angry and once admitted to the building, resented being ordered around by numerous policemen. The election committee finally asked the police to leave.

At first, Mayor Stapleton seemed to have a solid case. About seventy-five people testified that their signatures weren't valid because they were underage, or that they hadn't read or understood the petition and wanted their names removed from it. But then other witnesses were called. These stated that they had been offered money to repudiate their signatures or said they had been threatened if they did not ask for the removal of their names from the list.

It was pointed out that many of the errors in spelling and addresses that were "discovered," were not actually errors on the petition, but errors made by volunteers who had copied the information from the petition onto the cards that were used for follow-up investigation. The recall advocates also testified that their offices had been broken into and petitions and records were stolen.

The election committee made it known that they wanted to talk directly with Mayor Stapleton the next day. Suddenly the mayor was not to be found. It turned out that Stapleton had left on Saturday, May 31, after hearing that he would be called before the election commission. The attorney for those seeking the recall insisted that his defendants had the right to confront the complaining witness: Mayor Stapleton. Stapleton, however, stayed in Kansas City, ignoring telegrams asking him to return to Denver. It was only after the commission had ended its hearing that the mayor returned to Denver on June 7.

When the case was rested, Stapleton's group was able to throw out only a total of four hundred signatures of the more than sixteen thousand that they at first claimed were invalid. The backers of the petition maintained that they had more than enough qualified signatures to force an election. The election commission went into executive session, and after only an hour announced that the petition was legitimate and would be forwarded to the city council to call a special election.

The *Denver Post* labeled Stapleton's protest to the petition as "a fabrication of fraud, trickery, deception and misrepresentation." Faced with the commission's findings, Stapleton said he would turn to the federal courts, but he did not file suit. The city council set a recall election date of August 12.

Four candidates came forward to have their names appear on the ballot along with Stapleton's name for mayor. Only one contender posed a serious threat, the much disliked former mayor, Dewey Bailey. Voters faced a dilemma. Many thought they faced either voting for Bailey or voting for the Ku Klux Klan.

Municipal employees who wanted to keep their jobs had to report to precinct captains to assure that they and their families were registered to vote. The Klan came out in full force to support Ben Stapleton. Stapleton addressed a meeting of the Klan on July 14, 1924. In introducing him, the grand dragon of the Klan called for a few remarks from "Klansman Benjamin F. Stapleton, Mayor of Denver." In his short speech, Stapleton promised to work with the Klan and for the Klan. At rallies held elsewhere, however, Stapleton never mentioned the Klan.

Corporations and businessmen tended to support Stapleton. So did organized labor, which especially disliked Bailey because of his role in breaking a city streetcar strike. Some workers openly or secretly appreciated the KKK views against foreigners who they felt were taking jobs and lowering wages. When anti-Stapleton rallies were held, Klan members often attended and heckled and booed the speakers. Bailey spoke openly against the Klan, but on that issue, Stapleton remained silent.

A huge number of people registered to vote in the election, and with 119,000 voters on the books, it was the largest municipal election turnout Denver had ever seen. Stapleton easily won the election with twice the number of votes as the second-place candidate, Bailey. Stapleton made a brief victory statement saying that it was a triumph "for all those who are ready to work together for a better Denver." The grand dragon of the Colorado KKK, John Galen Locke, however, was not so modest. He met the press the next morning and claimed the victory for the Ku Klux Klan.

Under the Stapleton administration, laws were used to protect Klansmen and hurt anti-Klansmen. The bootleg squad was made up almost entirely of KKK members. The police used laws that allowed them to raid suspected stills and speakeasies and to invade the homes and businesses of anti-Klansmen. When patrolmen did confiscate whiskey, it seemed to "disappear" on its way to the storage vault. It was always missing when someone went to destroy it, and an unusually large number of confiscated bottles "fell" out of cars or were "smashed" when being unloaded on concrete floors. Members of the bootleg squad also seemed to have exceptionally fancy homes and cars. When patrolmen were accused of stealing liquor, the charges were always dropped. One argument was that since liquor was illegal, there were no property rights involved in stealing it.

The Klan prejudice against African Americans, Jews, and Catholics was evident in many ways. Besides incidents like the vetoing of the United Negroes Protective Association application to build a home for black seniors stating it would be a hazard to public health, members of the Junior Klan (for youth under the age of eighteen) openly mocked Jews and Catholics on school playgrounds, and complaining parents got little support.

Having done so well retaining Mayor Stapleton in Denver, the KKK turned its efforts toward winning at the state level. They succeeded in electing Clarence Morley as Governor of Colorado. Mayor Stapleton was one of the speakers at the deluxe banquet held for the new governor at the Brown Palace Hotel. Morley, like Stapleton, proved to be weak in office, easily bending to the wishes of the grand dragon of the Klan.

But on April 10, 1925, Mayor Stapleton made a bold move against the Klan. He gathered a handpicked strike force to hit stills, pool halls, and casinos in North Denver. The deputies hit sixty-eight targets and booked 189 prisoners. On Sunday, they pulled in another seventeen suspects. The next raid focused on the African American community. During the course of these raids, evidence exposed bribes for protection that involved the Klan and the police. It was estimated that during Stapleton's administration, $750,000 had been spent on police protection for illegal liquor establishments. Stapleton finally fired his police chief, Candlish, on July 15, 1925. This was almost the same time that the leader of the Colorado KKK lost his powerful position with the Klan and formed a new law and order group called the Minute Men.

Angry with Stapleton for betraying the Klan and exposing the corruption in the police force, the Minute Men started a second recall of Stapleton. The Minute Men argued that the current municipal government was clumsy. In the spring of 1926, they called for a special election to abolish the mayor's office altogether and to create a city manager form of government instead.

Ex-police chief Candlish backed this new proposal, which also called for a new city public service commission. Stapleton and his backers argued that the proposal for changing the form of government was not legitimate and that it infringed on city charter and state laws. The city council ruled that the measure was unconstitutional and refused to call a special election. The Colorado Supreme Court also condemned the measure.

By the end of the 1920s, the power of the KKK in Colorado was gone. Stapleton was defeated in his run for mayor in 1931, but shortly thereafter was elected as state auditor. He was elected mayor again in 1935, 1939, and 1943. During his last three terms as mayor, he played a leading role in creating the Denver Civic Center, the Denver mountain park system, the amphitheater at Red Rocks, the Valley Highway Project, and the Denver water system using funds available through the New Deal. He was a proponent of the Denver Municipal Airport, even when the newspapers referred to it as "Stapleton's Folly" out at "Rattlesnake Hollow." In 1944 that airport was named Stapleton International Airport. Today that site is referred to as the Stapleton neighborhood.

Ben Stapleton died on May 23, 1950. He could look back and claim many achievements for the city of Denver. But he would also have to acknowledge his first two terms as mayor, when he behaved like a jerk as a figurehead for the Ku Klux Klan.

SOURCES

Goodstein, Phil. *In the Shadow of the Klan: When the KKK Ruled Denver, 1920–1926.* Denver, CO: New Social Publications, 2006.

Time Magazine. "COLORADO: Interminable Ben," March 10, 1947.

John Galen Locke
COURTESY COLORADO HISTORICAL SOCIETY

CHAPTER 15

John Galen Locke

GRAND DRAGON OF THE KU KLUX KLAN

The reign of the Klan in Colorado was brief, but destructive. The Ku Klux Klan movement in the 1920s was nowhere near as violent as the Klan movement in the South immediately after the Civil War. But the 1920s Klan was an intimidating force in Colorado with political strength. Klansmen used fear, economic boycotts, and political pressure to further their agenda. Because they were hooded, considering themselves part of an "Invisible Empire," it was often difficult to pin specific acts of bigotry and violence on them. Individual Klansmen were hard to identify and seldom punished.

Shops owned by Jews and Catholics often failed or showed a huge drop in business due to KKK boycotting and threats. Klansmen went door-to-door advising businesses to fire black employees or face the consequences. In a show of solidarity, "klavalcades" of Klansmen in robes drove their cars through the main streets of cities such as Denver and Boulder, sometimes led by a thirty-five-piece Klan drum and bugle corps. Crosses were burned in public places to strike fear. The chief planner of the Colorado Klan was John Galen Locke, KKK grand dragon and ultimate jerk.

It was Veterans' Day in Denver, in the fall of 1924. Within a few minutes of each other, eleven crosses across the city lit up the night sky. They burned on the steps of the capitol, in Cheesman Park, and on Grasshopper Hill. Each cross stood fifteen to twenty-five feet high. They had been wrapped in burlap and soaked in kerosene. The burning crosses flared up at nine o'clock in the evening and lasted for about two hours.

Everyone knew the Ku Klux Klan was at work. Anti-Klansmen tried to extinguish the fires without success. Protestors of the cross burning demanded action from Denver officials. When the city council called the next day for an investigation, the police first said they had no evidence of any such crosses ever having been burned. Confronted with numerous eyewitnesses to the cross burnings, the police report was revised to state that the police were "unable to determine" who set the fires. There was no further follow-up. Only a few weeks later, crosses were burned all along the Front Range and in Clear Creek Canyon as a further demonstration of Klan strength.

The new Ku Klux Klan of the 1920s in Colorado was considerably different from the Klan that sprang up after the Civil War. The original Klan was an anti-black, white supremacist group founded mostly by Confederate soldiers and confined almost entirely to the South. That original group of Klansmen had almost disappeared by 1880.

The new Klan that was formed around 1915 in Georgia was opposed not only to blacks, but also to Jews, Catholics, Communists, and immigrants from eastern European or Mediterranean countries. Instead of being confined to the South, the new Klan was national. The men in the group professed to be patriots, in favor of law and order and fundamentalist Protestantism. By 1920, this new Klan boasted five million active members nationwide, with fifty thousand of these in Colorado.

The impetus for the 1920s Klan in Colorado began with the Denver Doers Club. Klan founder William J. Simmons came to Denver in April 1921. He had served in the Spanish-American War and was a friend of Leo Kennedy, a major in the Colorado National Guard. Simmons came to Denver to form a branch of the Klan. He held a meeting for retired veterans and other friends in a private room at the Brown Palace Hotel. They formed the Denver Doers Club or Citizens Doers Club, with the purpose of intervening in city life ostensibly to make Denver a better city.

In June of 1921 the Doers staged their first event: a midnight motorcade with hooded people in cars or on foot, demanding that movie theaters re-show what they regarded as a patriotic film that had had a short run because it had not been a box office success. There was some publicity surrounding this event, but no one suggested it was a Klan activity. It was not until January 1922 that the Doers Club announced itself as the Ku Klux Klan. They filed for incorporation with the secretary of state, and their request was granted.

Immediately the Klan movement in the state of Colorado was opposed by the National Association for the Advancement of Colored People (NAACP). Upon review, the KKK incorporation request was rejected on the basis of vague language. So the KKK, or "Nightriders" as they were sometimes called, although very active, remained unincorporated.

Under the leadership of Dr. John Galen Locke, Klaven No. 1 was formed in Denver. Longmont, Colorado, became the site for Klaven No. 2, and Boulder became Klaven No. 3. The movement spread and other groups were formed in Lafayette, Colorado Springs, Pueblo, Grand Junction, and Steamboat Springs. In addition to their bigotry regarding race, religion, and ethnicity, the group also opposed suggestive dances and titillating motion pictures. They wanted to abolish the civil service system, which they considered to be a refuge for Catholics, Jews, and the foreign born. In an effort to undermine Catholicism, they opposed the use of wine in church ceremonies.

There was a chapter of the Women of the Ku Klux Klan. Probably the biggest event that the women staged was on August 2, 1925, in Arvada. On that date, the group that some disparagingly called the "Kluckerettes" gathered and burned a cross in front of the Shrine of St. Ann. The event attracted between several hundred to several thousand women, depending on whose reports you read. However many attended, it alarmed the Catholic population of the Denver area. In response, on September 20, a pilgrimage assembled at Regis University and marched to the Shrine of St. Ann, where they conducted mass.

The key figure in the Klan movement in Colorado, Dr. John Galen Locke, was born in Port Henry, New York, in 1873. Locke desired to be a super patriot. His father had claimed that his fore-bears came over on the *Mayflower*, and Locke senior had served in the Union army during the Civil War. Locke decided he would fight for 100 percent Americanism through the Ku Klux Klan.

John Galen Locke moved to Colorado with his wife, Tessie, in 1893. During the Spanish-American War, Locke served in the Phil-ippines. After the war, he returned to Denver and earned a degree from the Denver Homeopathic College in 1904. In the fall of that year, Locke became an instructor at his alma mater and taught obstetrics. In 1909 he formed a medical practice with his father.

The more orthodox members of the medical community in Denver, disapproving of Locke's lack of medical education out-side of homeopathic training, did not think highly of the Lockes' medical practice, but the Lockes did well. Their waiting room was always full.

John Galen Locke was short, overweight, and sported both a mustache and goatee. Some new acquaintances were put off by the fact that wherever he went, Locke was usually accompanied by his three dogs: two Great Danes and a Dalmatian. In spite of these dis-advantages, John Galen Locke managed to fit in. He was an enthu-siastic joiner. In addition to medical associations, he joined the Elks and belonged to a number of groups such as the Denver Athletic Club, the Lakewood Country Club, and the Episcopal Church. The Colorado State Medical Society, however, rejected him.

In 1921 Locke added another group to his list; he became a member of the Denver Doers Club. The original nucleus of this group was veterans of the Spanish-American War. Both Locke and his father became members. After that club transformed into a full-blown Klan movement, Locke became the leader, or grand dragon, of the Klan for the state of Colorado with headquarters in the basement of his medical offices in Denver.

Locke shrewdly ran the "Kolorado Klan." Although there were sometimes impressive cross burnings and even a few bombings

along with other threatening vigilante activities, few acts of violence could actually be documented as the work of the Klan. Locke
viewed the Klan mainly as a way to gain power and political clout.
He became the master puppeteer behind many powerful political offices in the state of Colorado. Sometimes called "Dr. Rex," he
ruled like a king.

The sheeted members of the Klan drew attention to themselves. Seeking the support of Protestant churches to their cause,
it was not unusual in the middle of a service for several hooded
Klansmen to enter, walk forward to the altar, and place contributions from fifty to five hundred dollars near the pulpit. They
sought to build a good name with the parishioners.

Politicians who wanted Klan support on committees and in
elections were pressured to appoint Klansmen to key positions.
Some in the police department joined the Klan in what they saw
as a necessary step for career advancement. Soon some Denver
fire stations had a majority of Klansmen in their department.
These men then harassed Catholics and those who were not Klan
members to resign or transfer.

Labor leaders also learned the advantage of Klan support.
Pro-Klan men were appointed to political positions. The President
of the Colorado State Federation of Labor, Earle Hogue, was made
Denver city deputy treasurer while still keeping his union position. Others held dual roles in unions and in city hall.

After helping to elect Ben Stapleton as mayor of Denver in
1923, several Klan members were appointed to key positions in
Stapleton's administration, including that of Denver chief of police
and city attorney.

Locke often spoke at rallies. Some of these were held outside of Golden on top of South Table Mountain at an elevation
of 6,210 feet. Some people called this Castle Mountain and the
Klan referred to it as The Kastle. Starting in 1924, it was common
for Klansmen to gather there once or twice a week. Depending
on the event, between one thousand and ten thousand Klansmen
gathered. At the end of the ceremony, they burned giant crosses.

Guards were set up at the foot of the mountain to keep away non-members who might infiltrate and cause a disruption. Reports stated that non-Klansmen who tried to get into the event were often beaten before they were sent away.

Another favorite (indoor) gathering spot of the Klan was Cotton Mills Stadium. This was a T-shaped, two-story coliseum that had been an old, failed textile plant. The Klan purchased the building for around $60,000. They used the building for mass rituals, initiations, and celebrations. Sometimes the Klansmen went from the stadium to nearby Ruby Hill and burned crosses in the night.

As Colorado grand dragon, Locke was also sometimes called upon to speak at national meetings. A rousing speech he gave in Asheville, North Carolina, provoked various comments. One admirer called Locke "Buddha with a goatee," while a detractor referred to Locke as an "oversized Napoleon III."

By 1924 the Klan had considerable influence in the Republican Party in Denver. Locke handpicked Clarence Morley for the position of governor of Colorado, and Morley officially announced his candidacy in July of 1924. He ran on a strict "law and order" platform, and with the help of the Klan, was elected. Specially marked ballots were sent out advising people about candidates whom they should vote for to further Klan policies. Certain newspapers advocating other candidates or issues were boycotted.

In 1925 the *Rocky Mountain American* newspaper began publishing in Boulder. It advertised Klan-approved business firms. Ads in the paper would say "Kash and Karry groceries," or "Klothes Karefully Kleaned." A shop sold "Klassy Kut Klothes" so readers knew where they should shop. The newspaper published the following poem in its April 24, 1925 edition:

> *I would rather be a Klansman*
> *In robe of snowy white,*
> *Than to be a Catholic Priest*
> *In robe as black as night.*
> *For Klansman is AMERICAN*

and AMERICA is his home,
But a priest owes his allegiance
To a Dago Pope in Rome.

A parade of sixty cars and floats went down Pearl Street in Boulder in the winter of 1922. The licenses were draped so that the owners could not be identified. They carried signs that read 100 PER CENT AMERICANISM and JOIN THE INVISIBLE EMPIRE. Similar demonstrations took place in the nearby communities of Lafayette and Erie.

Some restaurants in Boulder put up signs saying they would not serve Jews or Catholics. Other restaurants said they served fish every day—except Friday—to drive Catholic business away. The editor of the rival newspaper, the *Boulder Daily Camera*, referred to the Klan as the "Komic Kapers Klub."

Clarence Morley extolled the virtues of the grand dragon of the Ku Klux Klan. The *Denver Express* quoted Morley on February 20, 1926, as saying, "In times of trouble the Almighty always sends some men to lead us. God sent us George Washington when we needed a leader in our struggle with England. God sent us Abraham Lincoln to preserve the union. And God has sent us John Galen Locke to lead our city out of its terrible condition of chaos and trouble."

It is estimated there were between three hundred and five hundred Klansmen in Boulder. There were probably fifty thousand Klansmen in Colorado. In the summer of 1925, Boulder's Klaven 3 hosted a convention of 2,500 Klan members from throughout the state.

In the 1924 general election, many factions were at work, and it was hard to determine which candidates might have the best chance at the office of mayor of Denver. It looked as if George Carlson might be a strong candidate, but labor forces refused to back him. Ben Stapleton emerged as a possibility. Stapleton pledged to enforce Prohibition laws, and this appealed to the Klan. Locke and the Klan quietly went to work to elect Stapleton. Stapleton managed to eke out a victory from a field of eight candidates. He appointed Rice Means, a Klansman, as city attorney and manager of safety. Through behind-the-scenes work, the Klan managed to elect a majority of members or sympathizers to the Colorado legislature, to put a friend in the governor's office, and to choose a Klansman as the U.S. senator from Colorado.

The police chief submitted his resignation three weeks after Stapleton took office, and Stapleton appointed a Klansman, William "Coca-Cola" Candlish as Denver's new police chief. Such appointments were always made in consultation with the grand dragon, John Galen Locke. Most people realized that Locke's office was the real city hall. Although not in the public eye as a major political force, through skillful planning, the Klan had achieved its political purposes.

John Galen Locke was in full control of the Klan in Colorado. He changed his basement at Glenarm Place into a makeshift auditorium. It included a bunker with a button-operated sliding steel door. The area was decorated with hunting trophies and weapons. Locke would sometimes receive visitors while seated on what looked like a throne. A gold seal of the United States was displayed above a fireplace. A vault held cash, guns, and ammunition.

Beginning in 1925, however, the Klan in Colorado fell on hard times. A recall effort mounted against Mayor Stapleton was narrowly defeated in spite of large infusions of Klan funds. Bowing to public pressure, Stapleton was forced to fire the Klansman police chief. Locke himself was charged with tax evasion and was briefly jailed.

The arrest of John Galen Locke was definitely a black eye for the Klan movement. The national headquarters in Atlanta sent their chief attorney to Denver. While the attorney praised Locke for being a "faithful servant of the order," Locke was told he had to leave his post as grand dragon. This did not sit well with many of the Colorado Klansmen. In fact, later investigations of the tax issue would prove that the allegations against Locke were groundless and that he had never used the Klan for personal enrichment.

At a hastily called Klan meeting the following day, there was great turmoil, with some suggesting that Locke should not resign and that the national office should be forced to take him back. Locke, however, tendered his resignation and waited. Some felt sure that Locke would be reinstated and that he would never form a rival group. Others thought Locke would quickly form a different group, separate from the Klan. Locke seemed to deliberately feed misinformation to both factions.

In the end, Locke organized a new group, Minute Men of America. Instead of wearing sheets, members wore uniforms that were copies of those worn by men in the American Revolution. Locke's break with the national headquarters caused the Colorado Klan to break into two groups. Twenty branches went with the new Minute Men organization while thirty-seven remained with the KKK. The Minute Men ran a newspaper called the *New American Patriot*. Some politicians, such as Mayor Stapleton, stuck with the Klan, while others, including a large number of the city council, went with the Minute Men.

The Minute Men set up an office close to Locke's medical clinic. Locke was installed as commander of the Minute Men on July 18, 1925, at the Cotton Mills Stadium. Since Locke had been in charge of smaller groups of the Klan in Utah, Nevada, and Idaho as well as Colorado, a few bands of Minute Men grew in those states, too. A small group of Minute Women also formed. But the Minute Men never took hold nationally. Members not only dwindled for the Minute Men but for the Klan as well.

The Minute Men group faded away completely in 1928. Locke was invited to return to a leadership position in what was a declining Colorado Klan, but he refused. Locke actively began to form yet another group to be called the Order of Equals with somewhat vague aims. It was a way to allow him to remain politically active and to continue to spew his bigotry under the guise of patriotism. Nothing much came of this group.

John Galen Locke died of a heart attack while attending a political meeting in the Brown Palace Hotel in 1935. He had lived to see the rise and fall of the KKK in Colorado, and by wielding his power as grand dragon of the Klan during much of the 1920s, he behaved like a jerk.

Sources

Dorsey, Larry. "Ku Klux Klan: The Invisible Empire in Boulder County." *Superior Historian* 6, no. 2 (August 2009).

Goodstein, Phil. *In the Shadow of the Klan: When the KKK Ruled Denver, 1920–1926.* Denver, CO: New Social Publications, 2006.

Lamm, Richard D., and Duane A. Smith. *Pioneers and Politicians: 10 Colorado Governors in Profile.* Boulder, CO: Pruett Publishing, 1984. Contains short chapters on ten important Colorado historical figures.

Noel, Thomas J. *Colorado Catholicism and the Archdiocese of Denver, 1857–1989.* Boulder, CO: University Press of Colorado, 1990. Now out of print, portions of the book can be read online.

Wood, Richard E. *Here Lies Colorado: Fascinating Figures in Colorado History.* Helena, MT: Farcountry Press, 2005.

CHAPTER 16

Governor Clarence Morley

THE ROAD TO LEAVENWORTH PRISON

*C*larence Morley was governor of Colorado from 1925 to 1927. His politics were simple and chilling. He was anti-foreigner, anti-Catholic, and anti-Jewish, so he appealed to the members of the Ku Klux Klan, who were strong forces in Colorado at the time.

Once elected, he proved ineffective. Although he had the power of the Klan behind him, his own party was split and he was vigorously opposed by the minority Democrats. Little was accomplished during his term of office, and his party did not choose to run him for another term. He did have enough time, however, to behave like a jerk, especially in his dealings with the University of Colorado and with Adams State College.

Seldom had a more splendid gathering taken place at Grand Central Station in Denver. It was the fall of 1927, and Imperial Wizard Hiram Evans, leader of all the Ku Klux Klans in the United States, was arriving. Waiting impatiently to greet him were the grand dragons from several states.

Amidst great pomp and ceremony, greetings were exchanged. As they left in a long motorcade, they were flanked by an escort of Denver police officers, treatment usually reserved for the highest of government officials. The impressive stream of cars made its way to the Brown Palace Hotel for a lavish celebration. Honored along with the imperial wizard were Clarence Morley, newly elected governor of Colorado, and the grand dragon of the KKK in Colorado, John Galen Locke. After being wined and dined, the imperial wizard went on to the Cotton Mills Stadium, which was packed with 35,000 Coloradans eager to hear him speak. The Klan in Colorado was at its zenith.

Governor Clarence Morley
COURTESY DENVER PUBLIC LIBRARY, WESTERN HISTORY COLLECTION

Many people think of the Ku Klux Klan as a phenomenon of the post–Civil War South. In fact, the greatest political successes of the Klan came in Colorado and Indiana during the 1920s. When World War I came to an end, there was still a distrust of "foreigners" and a strong anti-Communist attitude. There were frequent outbreaks of lawlessness and violence in Colorado cities. Inflation hit hard and raised suspicions about organized labor. During the summer of 1920, the employees of the Denver Tramway Company went on strike to protest wage cuts. Violence broke out and mobs poured into downtown Denver.

Citizens of Colorado found their earlier feelings of patriotism disappear in the difficult post-war years. In their place came feelings of fear. People feared the many examples they saw of increased crime, relaxed morals, and a drop in church attendance. They were upset with national scandals they read about. They sought for their state the leadership that they believed would take them back to traditional values. Mistakenly, they turned to the Ku Klux Klan to provide that leadership.

Minorities always suffer during times of mistrust; they also always bore the brunt of the Ku Klux Klan actions. Because there were a limited number of African Americans in the state, the main targets of the KKK in Colorado were Catholics, Jews, Italians, and eastern European immigrants. That made Clarence Morley a perfect candidate for the KKK to run for the governorship of the state. He increased his popularity among Republicans by adding to his campaign promises, including reducing government spending, helping farmers raise agricultural prices, and toughening the Prohibition laws.

Getting KKK support was essential to victory. As the *Denver Post* noted, "Beyond any doubt, the KKK is the largest and most cohesive, most efficiently organized political force in the state." For the 1924 governor's race, the *Denver Post* made no recommendation, saying that all the candidates were "awful."

The *Denver Express* on August 8, 1924, quoted Clarence Morley as saying, "Not for myself, mind you, do I wish to run, but for the benefit of the Klan." Members of the Klan packed the precinct caucuses of both the Republicans and the Democrats. They were most successful in the Republican Party. Although they often were unable to secure "first line placement on the ballot" for the names of their candidates, they were successful in getting their KKK people on the ballot.

To secure the necessary votes in the primary and general election, the Colorado Klan used "kluxing," which meant using recruiters, called "kleagles," to go across the state and secure support from voters. Many of these voters felt threatened in the post–World War I world. The Klan appealed with its promise of 100 percent Americanism, its strong support of Protestantism, and law and order. It even included a women's auxiliary, which worked diligently and was a particularly effective tool for garnering support.

Spreading the word also was a Ku Klux Klan newspaper called the *Rocky Mountain American*. It was headquartered in Boulder and published by William Francis. In addition to articles that supported the candidacy of Klan members such as Clarence Morley, the paper carried advertisements of businesses. Some of these used KKK-tinged catchphrases, such as a grocery that sold "Klean Kanned Goods" and a dealership that sold "Klean Klassy Kars."

The Ku Klux Klan was a big winner in the elections. It not only controlled the state assembly but also put Klansmen in the U.S. Senate and in the mayor's office. Most importantly, it elected Clarence Morley as governor of Colorado.

Clarence Morley was born in Dyerville, Iowa, on February 9, 1859. He attended public schools in Cedar Falls until his family moved to Trinidad, Colorado. It was in Colorado that Morley began his legal career as an official of the district court. Morley then attended law school at Denver University and carried on a private law practice for nineteen years.

Morley was active in the community, serving on the Denver School Board. In 1918 he was elected to serve on the bench of the Second Judicial Court in Denver and held this position until his Ku Klux Klan–endorsed run for governor in 1925.

The Klan in Colorado was led by Grand Dragon John Galen Locke. Locke did not run his group by trading on racism and resorting to acts of violence on individuals or private homes to cause upheaval in the community. Certainly there were a few such events. But for the most part, Locke chose to use the influence of the KKK to create a powerful political force in the state.

An example of the Klan's efficiency appeared during the Colorado primary election on September 9, 1924. Political volunteers placed pink tickets in the mailboxes and under doors of voters. These tickets listed every candidate as Protestant, Catholic, or Jew. Next to some of the Protestant names was an asterisk, which meant these candidates were unacceptable because they held close friendships with Catholics.

Under Locke's leadership, the Klan not only elected Clarence Morley as governor in 1924, but they also obtained a majority in the state House and Senate, elected the secretary of state, and secured a supreme court judgeship and seven benches on the Denver district court. They also claimed as Klan members the manager of safety, chief of police, city attorney, and many members of the city's police and fire departments.

Despite the Klan's climate of power, Morley's term as the twenty-fourth governor of the state of Colorado was not an easy one. There was a split in his own party and sharp opposition from the Democrats. As a result, almost all the Klan-sponsored legislation died in committee and never got to Governor Morley for his signature into law.

Shortly after being inaugurated as governor, Morley attempted to dismiss the adjutant general of the Colorado National Guard and two of his aides. His stated reason for doing this was "economy." The men refused to give up their positions and a district court invalidated the governor's orders. Morley did use his power as governor to make John Galen Locke an honorary colonel in the National Guard.

Because of Prohibition, Klan members in the state legislature introduced a bill to prohibit the use of sacramental wine, an obvious attack on Catholics. The new Republican, Klan-dominated legislature, with Morley's endorsement, attempted to abolish all state agencies except those created by the constitution. Civil liberties came under fire. A measure was introduced to ban marriage between Asians and whites. Another bill sought to prohibit drug addicts, drunks, epileptics, or persons charged with felonies from marrying. Yet another bill would repeal those laws that guaranteed public access to accommodations without regard for race or religion. During that session, 1,080 bills were introduced. The majority never got out of committee or reached the governor's office. Eighty-five percent of the bills went nowhere at all.

Not only were Democrats fighting against these bills, but so were a number of Republicans who were holdovers and not obligated in any way to the Klan. They continued to vote against Klan legislation. Every morning, an official KKK newspaper was placed on the desk of each of the legislators. On its front page it printed a daily Roll of Dishonor lisitng the names of those who had voted against Klan-sponsored legislation.

One area in which Morley was successful with state legislation was in strengthening Prohibition laws. Interestingly enough, this made him unpopular with a large segment of the population who believed that the police force was too vigorous and aggressive in enforcing Prohibition. He and the Klan also backed bills that would prohibit child labor and would guarantee a minimum wage to women.

Morley also was an advocate for prison reform. At one point during his two-year governorship, he suspended prison warden T. J. Tynan for refusing entry into the state prison to two physicians sent to examine prisoners after reported beatings and ill treatment by prison guards. Morley proved ineffective here also, because, notified of the suspension via telephone, Tynan ignored the executive order.

In spite of a few good pieces of legislation, Morley distinguished himself as a jerk in several ways. One of his most famous acts was his attempt to persecute the Jewish and Catholic professors at the University of Colorado in Boulder. As governor, Clarence Morley offered the president of the university all the money he needed to run that institution if he would "dismiss from the faculty and staff all the Roman Catholics and all of the Jews." In his famous stand for academic freedom, George Norlin, president of the University of Colorado, refused the governor's offer.

Billy Adams was a part of the Democratic minority in the legislature that fought Morley at every chance. He had thirteen Democratic senators supporting him and sometimes convinced Republicans who were not in the pocket of the Klan to join with him as well. Adams had to function in the upper house of the legislature where the Klan had a twenty-one to fourteen edge over him. He had the advantage of a detailed knowledge of senate rules, which he used to his advantage. Morley often lost to Billy Adams but got some satisfaction in the end by vetoing the $60,000 appropriation bill for the Normal School (Adams State College) when it reached his desk for signature. This was a big blow to Adams and his constituents in the San Luis Valley. The school managed to survive through donations and fundraising. In 1926 it was Adams who got some satisfaction. Morley did not get the Republican nomination for governor but lost out to Senator Rice Means. Billy Adams easily won the election and won the majority vote in fifty-nine of the sixty-three counties in the state of Colorado.

After Morley finished his one term as governor on January 11, 1927, he established C. J. Morley & Company. Morley had been the attorney in Colorado for a corporation called Investors Shares, Inc. Morley was one of its stockholders and a director. In this group he became associated with the men who later formed C. J. Morley & Company, a stock brokerage firm with its principal offices in Indianapolis.

Morley spent three years in Indiana getting his business well-established before he returned to Denver and started practicing law again.

In 1935 Clarence Morley was arrested for mail fraud. It was argued that his firm knowingly sent false statements in the mail in an attempt to defraud their customers. Morley was put on trial in Colorado and found not guilty. The federal courts then indicted him, and six others, on twenty-seven counts of mail fraud and accused him of using his prior connections as governor to defraud customers.

The charges against Morley and his company were that from the onset the company was involved in fraudulent transactions. They sold to customers various kinds of securities without delivering stocks. Many customers who invested lost money in Indiana, Ohio, and Kentucky. A raid was finally made on the company; some of the principals ran away and became fugitives from justice.

Morley did not deny that a fraudulent scheme was conceived and carried out using the U.S. mail. However his attorney in the appeal asserted that Morley had "impaired mental vigor and understanding," and that he could not be held responsible for what had happened. He also asserted that since Morley lived in Colorado, he was unaware of the bad acts being performed by his company in Indiana.

Morley was found guilty on one count and was sentenced to five years in Leavenworth Prison. The verdict was upheld when it was appealed by Morley's attorneys. He was the only one of the seven defendants in the fraud case to appeal.

In denying Morley's appeal, the court stated, "It is impossible to believe that defendant was not aware of the character and practices of his associates. The Morley Company's transactions covered eleven months and extended over a territory that included Ohio, Illinois, Kentucky, and Indiana. The utter absence of honesty and integrity in any of its activities during that period is significant."

After completing his prison term, Morley moved to Oklahoma City where he resided for three years before his death on November 15, 1948.

Clarence Morley was found by a jury of his peers to have deliberately defrauded a large number of investors. Long before this investment scheme, Morley behaved like a jerk in endorsing many bills that would limit the civil rights of Coloradans, by withholding funds from Adams State College, and by attempting to bribe the president of the University of Colorado by attaching a promise of funding to the dismissal of faculty and staff who were Jews or Catholics. In their profile of Morley, Lamm and Smith call him the "weakest and least appealing of all of Colorado's governors." Clarence Morley didn't accomplish much as governor, but while in office and later in his business dealings, he did show himself to be something of a jerk.

Sources

Carter, Carrol Joe. *Adams and the Ku Klux Klan*. Alamosa, CO: Adams State College, Division of Arts & Letters, Department of Government, 1980.

Dorsey, Larry. "Ku Klux Klan: The Invisible Empire in Boulder County." *Superior Historian* 6, no. 2 (August 2009).

Evening Independent, "Warden Ignores Executive Order to Leave Prison," January 5, 1927.

Hafnor, John. *Strange But True, Colorado: Weird Tales of the Wild West*. Fort Collins, CO: Lone Pine Productions, 2005. This book contains very short stories of many periods of Colorado history. It gives broad strokes but few details.

Jackson, Kenneth T. *The Ku Klux Klan in the City, 1915–1930*. New York: Oxford University Press, 1967. This book emphasizes that the Klan movement in the United States, especially in the 1920s, took a strong hold in cities as well as in rural areas.

Lamm, Richard D., and Duane A. Smith. *Pioneers and Politicians: 10 Colorado Governors in Profile*. Boulder, CO: Pruett Publishing, 1984.

CHAPTER 17

Captain Louis Scherf

THE COLUMBINE COAL STRIKE

*I*n the early 1900s in Colorado, small towns developed around mining operations. Many of these were company towns where a coal miner was given a place to live and could bring his wife and children. Sometimes the company built a small school and post office. Miners were often paid in script that could only be used in the company store rather than cash.

Wages were low and safety issues were ignored. The unorganized miners were helpless. Conditions were ripe for organized labor to gather enough members to demand better working conditions. If a strike was threatened, guards, militia, or state police were brought in.

One of these small company towns was Serene, Colorado. When men began to organize to try to achieve better working conditions, Captain Louis Scherf arrived on the scene to keep the miners in line. In true jerk fashion, he did not hesitate to use force, including bullets, against even unarmed miners and their wives.

It was almost daybreak on November 21, 1927, when about five hundred striking miners tramped up to the gates of the Columbine Mine property at Serene, Colorado. Scattered among them were a few women, supporting their husbands' demands for higher wages and better working conditions. Behind the gates stood mine guards and local law enforcement officials, including Deputy Sheriff Lou Beynan of Weld County.

Also standing in wait was Captain Louis Scherf with his Colorado state police, who were sometimes referred to as Rangers. Captain Scherf faced the mob and demanded to know who their leaders were. The strikers shouted in reply, "We are all leaders."

Scherf told the men they would not be allowed on company property. The strikers insisted they had a right to continue on down the road that led to the school and to the post office. When the mob of miners surged forward, Captain Scherf shot a pistol into the air twice, the signal for the Rangers to fire into the crowd. In addition to handguns, some reports indicate that two machine guns were also turned on the miners. It became the Columbine Mine Massacre.

There were already several little mining towns in the Northern Colorado coalfields including Erie, Superior, Louisville, and Lafayette. In addition to the mine company store, several groceries and shops were in operation in these small towns. In 1905 three new communities were established along the tracks of the Union Pacific Railroad. These were Dacono, Frederick, and Firestone. Serene was another small coal-mining town belonging to the Rocky Mountain Fuel Company and located just east of Erie. It was surrounded by a fence and contained houses for miners, a school, a post office, and a company store.

In the mid 1920s, Colorado was the number one coal-producing state west of the Mississippi River. But wages paid in Colorado were lower than those paid to miners in nearby unionized states such as Wyoming and Montana. Colorado miners also did not benefit from new equipment and techniques such as using machines instead of men to wield shovels for loading coal. Long hours, low wages, hard work, and no bargaining power meant that conditions in the northern Colorado coal mines were ripe for a big unionizing effort.

Because of recent bloody events that followed the coal miners' strike at Ludlow, Colorado, the United Mine Workers of America was not looking for another major union effort in the state. That opened the way for a different union to move onto the Colorado scene. The Industrial Workers of the World (IWW), often called the "Wobblies," were ready to step in and try to organize the miners. Unions were generally not in favor in the United States during the 1920s. This union in particular was regarded with considerable doubt and distrust by many people, since it was thought that the IWW members included too many foreigners and socialists.

IWW organizers tended to stand on street corners on soap boxes and recruit new members. To curb this, in 1912, Denver passed a law prohibiting soapbox speeches. Everyone was aware that this law was aimed specifically at silencing the IWW efforts to organize, but the law just galvanized more union organizers to action. Many more Wobblies came pouring into Denver. They talked on street corners and consequently were thrown in jail. No sooner was one Wobblie taken away, than another took his place. As soon as one was released from jail, he went straight to the nearest corner and began talking again. These union organizers kept the police busy and the city jails overcrowded. Eventually Denver was forced to repeal the ordinance.

A few Wobblie symbols were evident even at the ill-fated Ludlow strike in southern Colorado, although it was definitely a United Mine Workers union strike. After that strike was broken and the workers and union realized they had failed there, the IWW continued to try to recruit members. They welcomed unskilled workers to their ranks. The IWW brought blacks, whites, Asians, and Hispanics into the same local union groups. The United Mine Workers of America opposed most of the activities of the Wobblies as well as their Socialist agenda. They considered them to be rivals rather than allies.

On October 18, 1927, the Colorado coal miners, under the banner of the IWW, went on strike. By the first of November, twelve thousand miners were idle. All of the mines in the Northern Field were closed except for the Columbine Mine. The miners who were out on strike were not supported by pension funds or unemployment checks. They somehow survived by eating a lot of canned pinto beans and little else. They seldom even had bread. Sometimes their food was supplemented when a team of miners went out and hunted jackrabbits and cottontails. The group that was sent out hunting might bring back two or three hundred rabbits, which were then taken to the community hall and passed out to the striking miners.

The Colorado militia had been disbanded after the violent events that occurred during the Ludlow strike. Now it appeared that with unrest in the coalfields, troops might be needed again. The Colorado National Guard had been established in July 1917, but Governor William "Billy" Adams didn't want to use the Guard against the coal miners. Instead he set up an additional military force called the "state law enforcement department." Others often referred to them as the Colorado state police or Rangers. To head the group, he named Captain Louis N. Scherf.

Louis Scherf had been a regular soldier in the army from 1910 to 1913, leaving the service as a sergeant. He then went to officer's training school at Fort Riley, Kansas, before entering World War I in 1917, commissioned as a captain. After the war, he worked as an investigator for the Denver district attorney. During the 1922 coal strike, Scherf had served under Colonel Pat Hamrock, who was one of the two men in charge of the militia at Ludlow. Once he was appointed chief of the new law enforcement department, Scherf trained his twenty men at Walsenburg and supplied each of them with riot guns, automatic revolvers, and canisters of tear gas. Using Prohibition laws, Captain Scherf's men often harassed IWW members by searching their homes under the pretext of looking for illegal liquor.

On November 5, mine guards, officers, and strikers met and clashed in Berwind Canyon. The strikers, under the banner of the IWW, were marching toward a Colorado Fuel and Iron (CF&I) mine to hold a demonstration. Their goal was also the old Berwind jail where they hoped to free some union men who had been locked up for their union activities by Marshal Sanders. It was common for the police to jail union organizers and then to move them quickly from jail to jail so that IWW lawyers could not locate them to represent them.

About five hundred strikers participated in the march. They were met by Captain Louis Scherf and his men, who had lined up across the road at a bridge. Several fights broke out, and although Scherf's men had pistols as well as pick handles, they did not shoot. Scherf and his men used admirable restraint even though they were provoked and humiliated by taunts from the mob.

Two famous women were involved in this march. One was called Santa Benash. She was six feet tall, weighed 235 pounds, and was sometimes called "The Amazon." Also in the crowd was Santa Benash's sister, Amelia "Milka" Sablich, who often wore red to stand out in the crowd and was called "Flaming Milka." Both women dove into the fight with fists flying. A mounted mine guard rode Amelia Sablich down, grabbed her by the hand, and dragged her along, breaking her wrist. She was handcuffed that day and after the fight was taken to Trinidad where she was jailed.

The crowd of striking miners pushed the guards and state police back and headed for the mine. Captain Scherf and his men passed them and reached the mine first. When the strikers arrived at the mine, they planned to hold a demonstration. Captain Scherf and his men prevented this. Every time speakers got up to the platform to address the crowd, the guards and state police pulled them down. Finally the strikers left, vowing to return on Sunday.

On Sunday, however, instead of returning to Berwind, the strikers met at Ludlow. Four patrol planes of the National Guard spotted the gathering crowd of men. The planes dived and swooped down on the strikers. Although they did not shoot, their flying so close frightened the strikers into leaving and seeking cover.

Captain Louis Scherf and his men kept busy. On November 7, he led a midnight raid on the IWW headquarters in Walsenburg. They wrecked the place and arrested over a dozen strike leaders. Governor Adams declared that the IWW was an "un-American organization," and said that he would strictly enforce the state's anti-picketing laws.

At this time, the general public was solidly against the strikers. An example of this can be seen from a newspaper editorial published in the *Boulder Daily Camera* on November 17, 1927. It read, "Machine guns are the best answer to picketers. Posted at the Columbine Mine, willing workers go to work while picketers slink back. Machine guns manned by willing shooters are wanted at other Colorado mines . . ."

A similar attitude and tone was evident in an editorial in the *Denver Morning Post* that appeared two weeks before the Columbine Mine shootings: "The IWW . . . precipitated the strike without justification and without notice. That such a group made up of outlaws and foreigners . . . should be permitted to do its war dance without molestation at the expense of the remainder of the state is outrageous."

Due to the strike, coal was in short supply in Colorado. Almost every coal mine in the state was closed except for the Columbine Mine. The warden of the Colorado penitentiary needed coal for the prison and the Colorado state hospital. The warden found his own solution. The Cuckoo Coal Mine was located in Canon City. The warden sent twenty-one of his convicts there to dig coal. They were able to bring out about twelve tons of coal a day for use at the prison and the hospital.

In addition to militia, planes were sometimes used to help stifle mine demonstration. On November 16, National Guard airplanes flew over the coal mines. Those on the ground could see that machine guns had been mounted on the planes. Patrol flights went up at two-hour intervals all day long to keep any gathering of miners under surveillance.

On November 17, there was a big parade in Serene near the Columbine Mine. A caravan of about five hundred automobiles carrying strikers arrived. The first car was an open touring car, and standing in it, wearing a red dress, was none other than Milka Sablich, waving an American flag. She had joined this group as soon as she was released from the Trinidad jail.

Many children and their mothers sneaked into the parade. Some miners brought along musical instruments and members of the group sang. Mugs of hot coffee and doughnuts were given to the crowd. These were provided by the new dominant stockholder in the mine, Josephine Roche.

Captain Louis Scherf and his men arrived at the Columbine Mine on November 20. Scherf spent the day checking gates, fences, and big metal sheets that had been made in the mine shop and put up in front of offices and equipment as protection for the guards. He also sent to Denver that night and secured steel helmets for his men to wear.

A public road went through the area and led to a school and a post office. Previously Columbine General Manager Merle Vincent had ordered that this road was to remain open, and that guards never were to shoot at strikers even if it meant destruction of mine property. These directives came from Josephine Roche. She was the daughter of John Roche, founder of the Rocky Mountain Fuel Company who had recently died, and she was now the major stockholder. She had different ideas about how the mine should be run. When Merle Vincent learned that state militia were on the mine property, he became concerned since his boss had made it very clear that the miners were not to be fired upon.

Merle Vincent went to Denver and met Governor Adams at the Brown Palace Hotel to ask that the police force be moved from the mine property. The governor admitted that he was unaware that Scherf and his men had moved to the Columbine Mine, and said he had not given orders for that action. The governor said he would contact Scherf and order him to depart.

Apparently, Governor Adams did try to contact Captain Scherf, but was unsuccessful. It seemed that every time the governor called, Captain Scherf was "out." Sensing that trouble was ahead, the governor did send some members of the Industrial Commission to go to the Columbine Mine and investigate.

On November 21, approximately five hundred miners, and about fifty of their wives, marched up to the north gate of the Columbine Mine property. The miners were met by county law enforcement officials, company guards, and Captain Scherf, though Scherf and his men were not wearing uniforms. They stood behind the first of two fences that surrounded the property.

Up to this point in time at the Columbine Mine, although there was tension, the strike had been a pretty friendly affair. Today would be different. Instead of just company guards, Scherf and his Rangers were there. A Weld County deputy sheriff who knew many of the miners and their families warned them and begged the strikers not to enter the company property.

The strikers were unarmed. Many, however, carried the American flag. The symbolic display of American flags seemed central in these demonstrations. The strikers insisted that they were citizens with rights. The flags were an irritation to those opposed to the strike.

Initially, at the first fence gate, there was simply some shoving and name calling. One of the strike leaders, Adam Bell, stepped up to the gate and ordered that it be unlocked. As Adam Bell went over or through the gate, three Rangers began clubbing him until he fell unconscious to the ground. Other miners pushed their way forward and tried shielding him, including a woman who was one of the flag bearers.

The angry and desperate miners surged through the gate and tore down the fence. Fights broke out. Immediately mine guards began beating the miners with clubs and pipes. Tear gas was thrown into the crowd. Miners used fists and threw rocks at the guards and Rangers, who were wearing their steel helmets. In the face of this crowd, the guards and militia retreated about 120 yards to another fence.

It was then that Captain Louis Scherf shot his gun twice into the air, apparently the signal to begin firing. The state police began shooting automatic pistols, rifles, and riot guns, and threw gas grenades at the miners. Many of the miners at the scene later reported that at least two and possibly three 30-caliber machine guns were also used.

As chaos broke out, the miners ran, trying to escape the gunfire. Some miners fled to nearby houses. Six strikers were killed and more than sixty more were wounded including at least two women. It was probably no accident that the flag carried by Jerry

David was found to have seventeen bullet holes in it. The injured were left on the road. Later, strikers carrying a white flag of truce were allowed to pick up the dead and wounded.

The injured were taken to doctors and hospitals in Erie, Boulder, and Longmont. Colonel Paul Newlon of the National Guard rushed from the scene to Denver, and by seven-thirty that morning had reported the event to Governor Adams. The governor immediately issued a press report blaming the miners for the killings. He said, "My reports show conclusively that the strikers were to blame for Monday's affair." He added, "Scherf exercised great patience and wonderful courage, doing everything possible to prevent bloodshed."

After the event, which quickly took on the name of the Columbine Mine Massacre, miners gathered in Erie outside the doctor's office where many of the dead were brought and where several of the wounded were treated. Then funerals for the victims began. On Wednesday, one man was buried, and on Thursday another. The last victims were buried on Friday, Thanksgiving Day. It is estimated that three thousand miners from throughout the state arrived at the funerals to pay their respects. Coal miners, in the course of their careers, moved about a great deal, often working in a dozen Colorado mines, so they had relatives and friends in many different mining camps.

Newspapers carried reports of the events that occurred at the mine. The guards and Rangers continued to deny that machine guns were used, but two days after the demonstration, the *Rocky Mountain News* showed a photo of a machine gun at the Columbine Mine mounted high on the mine tipple, a structure where normally coal was loaded onto railroad cars. The mounted gun was ready for action.

Other papers also issued reports of what really had occurred that day. These editors spoke out at their own risk. A month after the strike, Frank Palmer, the founding editor of the *Colorado Labor Advocate*, was arrested at a meeting in Longmont and held for over two weeks before he was released. The following month, he was arrested again for speaking in Lafayette.

Governor Adams finally declared a state of insurrection in Boulder and Weld Counties and ordered out the Colorado National Guard to occupy the Northern Fields. Adjutant General Newton used the proclamation of martial law to send for militia, tanks, and a medical unit. This was a force of 325 men, supported by forty-five cavalry and two tanks. Airplanes continued to patrol while Governor Adams pronounced the area to be in a state of insurrection. Guardsmen were posted at the Puritan, Grant, and Monarch Mines. Passes were required to get in and out of the mines and a curfew was imposed.

As news of the Columbine Mine shootings circulated among all the Colorado coal mines, many workers wanted to gather, return armed, and shoot it out with the guards and the Rangers, but the IWW officials managed to argue against this and prevail.

Adam Bell, who was perceived to be the IWW strike leader, was jailed without charges. A federal district court judge eventually ordered the state to release Bell. Even after that decision, Bell was held an additional four days. Several other unionists were convicted of vagrancy and sentenced to ninety days in jail.

In the days that followed, the Weld County coroner impaneled a jury. As would be expected, there were conflicting reports of what had happened. The state police testified they had not used machine guns, even as some miners identified the guard who had climbed to the tipple and operated the machine gun that was mounted there. Another machine gun was reported to have been manned by one of Scherf's Rangers.

The mine operators insisted that the miners were armed and were shooting at the guards and militia. All the miners said that their leader, Adam Bell, had insisted that all weapons had to be checked in at the miners' meeting place in Erie before the march to the mine. County Deputy Sheriff William Wyatt from Greeley reported that he did not see any miner fire a weapon. Perhaps the most significant testimony is the fact that no policemen were shot. The only wounded guard had apparently injured his thumb against a fence. There were seven hours of testimony, but it took the jury just thirty minutes of deliberation to reach their verdict.

The jury's decision was that the strikers had died after having been properly and legally warned not to enter the mine property. They had been shot by persons unknown who were lawful officers of the state of Colorado and the deaths were not "felonious." Governor Adams absolved Captain Scherf and the Rangers of any wrongdoing and said they acted in self-defense. By Thanksgiving the investigation was over and the officers who fired on the miners were exonerated. With this verdict and many of the IWW leaders in jail, it seemed that the strike had failed and was over.

Roadblocks were set up preventing other IWW members from entering southern Colorado through New Mexico. In January, nineteen IWW leaders who had been jailed in Walsenburg were driven to the New Mexico border, released, and told to walk south. They were not to come back to Colorado under penalty of death.

The State Federation of Labor offered to mediate the strike and the State Industrial Commission called a hearing into the miners' grievances. The committee set up hearings on January 12. About seven hundred strikers marched down Main Street. One of these strikers shot and wounded a policeman. The strikers then fled into the IWW hall. That afternoon, the state police stormed the hall. Two strikers were shot and killed, the hall was shot up, and the IWW papers were taken outside and burned. This time the jury found that the state police were responsible for the deaths that had occurred and recommended further investigation. That never happened.

On February 28, 1928, the mine operators offered an armistice, and many men went back to work. They won a dollar a day pay raise.

There were significant changes at Rocky Mountain Fuel with Josephine Roche in control. Roche was a Vassar graduate and a liberal Democrat, but even she wanted nothing to do with the IWW, a group that she thought was too radical. Instead, she announced that she would sign a contract with the United Mine Workers union. In May 1928, the Rocky Mountain Fuel Company signed a contract with the United Mine Workers of America. This contract raised the miners' pay, began to modernize the equipment, and made other concessions. The contract was worded following the pattern of the Declaration of Independence and was perceived as a document of independence for coal miners in Colorado.

Josephine Roche probably was fully aware of what would follow. Rockefeller's CF&I did not sign the agreement and went about putting the Rocky Mountain Fuel Company out of business. They undersold Rocky Mountain Fuel Company coal, and local banks refused to provide financing for the Roche company. The United Mine Workers union even invested in the company, and during the Depression, the workers voluntarily cut their wages. Still, the Rocky Mountain Fuel Company eventually had to file for bankruptcy.

Immediately after the inquest into the incidents that occurred at the Columbine Mine, Captain Louis Scherf and his men were transferred back to the Southern Coal Fields. Although Scherf had been cleared of all wrongdoing, and indeed was commended for his part in the Columbine Mine affair, he clearly was not comfortable with the situation. It was rumored that he tried to get an accusation filed against himself so that there could be a trial and he could be officially declared innocent.

Scherf knew that there is no time limit to a charge of murder, and he knew that you could not be tried twice for the same crime. Although the coroner's jury had absolved him and his men of guilt, and the chairman of the Industrial Commission had praised him, Scherf still wanted a trial. He felt that in the current political climate, he would be certain to be found innocent. He feared that officials friendly to the miners might one day be in power, and that if he were tried then for his part in the mine massacre, he might well be found guilty. Whether guilty of a crime or not, Scherf knew that he had behaved like a jerk.

SOURCES

Foner, Philip S. *History of the Labor Movement in the United States, Volume IV: The Industrial Workers of the World, 1905–1917.* New York: International Publishers, 1965.

May, Lowell, and Richard Myers, eds. *Slaughter in Serene: the Columbine Coal Strike Reader.* Denver, CO: Bread and Roses Workers' Cultural Center, 2005. One of the few detailed accounts of the events at Serene, sponsored and printed by a worker's group.

Sampson, Joanna. *Walking Through History on Marshall Mesa.* Boulder, CO: City of Boulder Open Space Department, 1995. A pamphlet filled with good local information.

Smith, Phyllis. *Once a Coal Miner. The Story of Colorado's Northern Coal Field.* Boulder, CO: Pruett Publishing, 1989.

BIBLIOGRAPHY

Armitage, Susan, and Elizabeth Jameson. *The Women's West*. Norman, OK: University of Oklahoma Press, 1987.

Bancroft, Caroline. *Augusta Tabor: Her Side of the Scandal*. Boulder, CO: Johnson Publishing Co., 1961.

―――. *Estes Park and Trail Ridge: Their Dramatic History*. Boulder, CO: Johnson Publishing Co., 1967.

―――. *Tabor's Matchless Mine and Lusty Leadville*. Boulder, CO: Johnson Publishing Co., 1960.

―――. *Trail Ridge Country*. Boulder, CO: Johnson Publishing Co., 1968.

Bird, Isabella. *A Lady's Life in the Rocky Mountains*. London: Virago, 1982.

Buchholtz, C. W. *Rocky Mountain National Park: A History*. Boulder, CO: Colorado Associated University Press, 1983.

Burton, Doris Karen. *Queen Ann Bassett*. Vernal, UT: Burton Enterprises, 1992.

Butler, Anne M. *Daughters of Joy, Sisters of Misery: Prostitutes in the American West, 1865–90*. Chicago: University of Illinois Press, 1985.

Carlson, Chip. *Tom Horn: "Killing Men Is my Specialty . . .": The Definitive History of the Notorious Wyoming Stock Detective*. Cheyenne, WY: Beartooth Corral, 1991,

Carlson, Chip, and Larry D. Ball. *Tom Horn: Blood on the Moon: Dark History of the Murderous Cattle Detective*. Glendo, WY: High Plains Press, 2001.

Carter, Carrol Joe. *Adams and the Ku Klux Klan*. Alamosa, CO: Adams State College, Division of Arts & Letters, Department of Government, 1980.

Churchill, E. Richard. *Doc Holliday, Bat Masterson, and Wyatt Earp*. Leadville, CO: Timberline Books, 1974.

Clifford, Howard. *The Skagway Story*. Anchorage, AL: Alaska Northwest Publishing Co., 1975.

Coel, Margaret. *Chief Left Hand*. Norman, OK: University of Oklahoma Press, 1981.

Collier, William Ross, and Edwin Victor Westrate. *The Reign of Soapy Smith, Monarch of Misrule, in the Last Days of the Old West and the Klondike Gold Rush*. Garden City, New York: Doubleday, Doran & Company, 1935.

Couch, Jacqualine Grannell. *Those Golden Girls of Market Street: An Historical Glimpse*. Fort Collins, CO: Old Army Press, 1974.

Craig, Reginald S. *The Fighting Parson: The Biography of Colonel John M. Chivington*. Tucson, AZ: Westernlore Press, 1994.

Donnel, James E. *The Military Career of John M. Chivington: A Thesis*. Laramie, WY: University of Wyoming, 1960.

Dorsey, Larry. "Ku Klux Klan: The Invisible Empire in Boulder County." *Superior Historian* 6, no. 2 (August 2009).

Dumett, Raymond E., ed. *Mining Tycoons in the Age of Empire, 1870–1945*. Burlington, VT: Ashgate Publishing Co., 2009.

Dunn, William R. *I Stand By Sand Creek*. Fort Collins, CO: Old Army Press, 1985.

Dunning, Harold M. *The Life of Rocky Mountain Jim (James Nugent)*. Boulder, CO: Johnson Publishing Co., 1967.

Enss, Chris. *Pistol Packin' Madams: True Stories of Notorious Women of the Old West.* Guilford, CT: Globe Pequot Press, 2006.

Evening Independent, "Warden Ignores Executive Order to Leave Prison," January 5, 1927.

Fenwick, Robert W. *Alfred Packer: The True Story of Colorado's Man-Eater.* Lake City, CO: The Timberline Craftsman, 1989.

Floyd, E. Randall. *The Good, the Bad, and the Mad: Weird People in American History.* Augusta, GA: Harbor House, 1999.

Foner, Philip S. *History of the Labor Movement in the United States, Volume IV: The Industrial Workers of the World, 1905–1917.* New York: International Publishers, 1965.

Goodstein, Phil. *In the Shadow of the Klan: When the KKK Ruled Denver, 1920–1926.* Denver, CO: New Social Publications, 2006.

Hafnor, John. *Strange But True, Colorado: Weird Tales of the Wild West.* Fort Collins, CO: Lone Pine Productions, 2005.

Hoig, Stan. *The Sand Creek Massacre.* Norman, OK: University of Oklahoma Press, 1961.

Jackson, Kenneth T. *The Ku Klux Klan in the City, 1915–1930.* New York: Oxford University Press, 1967.

Jessen, Kenneth. *Bizarre Colorado: A Legacy of Unusual Events and People.* Loveland, CO: J. V. Publications, 1994.

———. *Colorado Gunsmoke: True Stories of Outlaws and Lawmen on the Colorado Frontier.* Boulder, CO: Pruett Publishing, 1986.

———. *Colorado's Strangest: A Legacy of Bizarre Events and Eccentric People.* Loveland, CO: J. V. Publications, 2005.

Johnson, Marilynn S. *Violence in the West*. Boston: Bedford/St. Martin's, 2009.

Karsner, David. *Silver Dollar: The Story of the Tabors*. New York: Crown Publishers, 1932.

Krakel, Dean F. *The Saga of Tom Horn*. Lincoln, NE: University of Nebraska Press, 1954.

Kushner, Ervan F. *Alferd G. Packer, Cannibal! Victim?* Frederick, CO: Platte 'N Press, 1980.

Lamm, Richard D., and Duane A. Smith. *Pioneers and Politicians: 10 Colorado Governors in Profile*. Boulder, CO: Pruett Publishing, 1984.

Laughlin, Rosemary. *The Ludlow Massacre of 1912–14*. Greensboro, NC: Morgan Reynolds Publishing, 2006.

May, Lowell, and Richard Myers, eds. *Slaughter in Serene: the Columbine Coal Strike Reader*. Denver, CO: Bread and Roses Workers' Cultural Center, 2005.

MacKell, Jan. *Brothels, Bordellos, and Bad Girls: Prostitution in Colorado 1860–1930*. Albuquerque, NM: University of New Mexico Press, 2004.

McClure, Grace. *The Bassett Women*. Athens, OH: Ohio University Press, 1984.

Marshall, James. *Santa Fe: The Railroad that Built an Empire*. New York: Random House, 1945.

Martelle, Scott. *Blood Passion: The Ludlow Massacre and Class War of the American West*. New Brunswick, NJ: The Rutgers University Press, 2007.

Mendoza, Patricia. M. *Song of Sorrow: Massacre at Sand Creek*. Denver, CO: Willow Wind Publishing Co., 1993.

Mills, Enos. *Early Estes Park*. Estes Park, CO: Denver, CO: Big Mountain Press, 1963.

Monaghan, Jay, and Larry D. Ball. *Tom Horn: Last of the Bad Men*. Lincoln, NE: University of Nebraska Press, 1946.

Monnet, John B., and Michael McCarthy. *Colorado Profiles: Men and Women Who Shaped the Centennial State*. Niwot, CO: University Press of Colorado, 1996.

Myers, John. *Doc Holliday*. Boston: Little, Brown, & Co., 1955.

Noel, Thomas J. *Colorado Catholicism and the Archdiocese of Denver, 1857–1989*. Boulder, CO: University Press of Colorado, 1990.

Obmascik, Mark. *Halfway to Heaven*. New York: Free Press, 2009.

O'Connor, Richard. *Bat Masterson*. Garden City, NY: Doubleday & Co., 1957.

Papanikolas, Zeese. *Buried Unsung: Louis Tikas and the Ludlow Massacre*. Lincoln, NE: University of Nebraska Press, 1982.

Pickering, James H. *This Blue Hollow*. Boulder, CO: University Press of Colorado, 1999.

Pryor, Alton. *Bawdy House Girls: A Look at the Brothels of the Old West*. Roseville, CA: Sagebrush Publishing, 2006.

Richmond, Patricia Joy. *Trail to Disaster*. Denver, CO: Colorado Historical Society, 1990.

Rutter, Michael. *Upstairs Girls: Prostitution in the American West*. Helena, MT: Farcountry Press, 2005.

Sampson, Joanna. *"Remember Ludlow!"* Denver, CO: Colorado Historical Society, 1999.

———. *Walking Through History on Marshall Mesa*. Boulder, CO: City of Boulder Open Space Department, 1995.

Seagraves, Anne. *Soiled Doves: Prostitution in the Early West.* Hayden, ID: Wesanne Publications, 1994.

Shirley, Gayle C. *More than Petticoats: Remarkable Colorado Women.* Guilford, CT: Globe Pequot Press, 2002.

Schott, Bob. *Blood at Sand Creek: The Massacre Revisited.* Caldwell, ID: Caxton Printers, 1994.

Simmons, Virginia McConnell. *The San Luis Valley: Land of the Six Armed Cross*, 2nd ed. Niwot, CO: University of Colorado Press, 1999.

Smith, Duane A. *Horace Tabor: His Life and the Legend.* Niwot, CO: University Press of Colorado, 1989.

Smith, Phyllis. *Once a Coal Miner. The Story of Colorado's Northern Coal Field.* Boulder, CO: Pruett Publishing, 1989.

Spence, Mary Lee, ed. *The Expeditions of John Charles Frémont, Vol. 3, Travels from 1848–1854.* Chicago: University of Chicago Press, 1984.

Stein, Leon, and Philip Taft, eds. *Massacre at Ludlow: Four Reports.* New York: Arno Press, 1971.

Tarasenko, Kathryn. *The Media on the Ludlow Massacre: Objective Witness or Tool of Government and Big Business?* Greeley, CO: University of Northern Colorado Thesis, College of Arts & Sciences, Department of Journalism and Mass Communication, May 1996.

Time Magazine. "COLORADO: Interminable Ben," March 10, 1947.

Wheeler, Richard S. *Snowbound.* New York: Tom Doherty Associates, 2010.

Williamson, Ruby G. *From Kansas to the Matchless: A Tabor Story 1857–1880.* Gunnison, CO: B & B Printers, 1975.

Winford, Jessica L. *An Analysis of Ivy Lee's Handling of the Ludlow Massacre: An Application of Grunig's Models of Public Relations.* Greeley, CO: University of Northern Colorado, College of Arts & Sciences, Department of Journalism and Mass Communication, 2003.

Wommack, Lindar. *Our Ladies of the Tenderloin: Colorado's Legends in Lace.* Caldwell, ID: Caxton Press, 2005.

Wood, Richard E. *Here Lies Colorado: Fascinating Figures in Colorado History.* Helena, MT: Farcountry Press, 2005.

INDEX

INDEX

L

La Glorieta Pass, 20–21, 23
Lail, William, 174–75
Lamb, Elkanah J., 36, 39, 46
Lawson, John, 164–65
Leadville, Colorado, 97–98, 107
LeFors, Joe, 137–38
Left Hand (Arapaho), 15, 18–19,
    24–25
Lewis, Charles, 172
Lewis, William, 135
Light, John, 112
Lincoln, Abraham, iii, 31
Linderfeldt, Lt. Karl, vi, 153, 157,
    159–60, 163–65
Lindsey, Henry, 170
Lippiatt, Gen., 156, 159
Little Pittsburgh silver mine, 98
Little Raven (Arapaho), 19, 24
Locke, John Galen, v, 172–73, 177,
    180, 181, 183–90, 191, 194–95
Locke, Tessie, 184
Los Pinos Indian Agency, 53, 57
Louderback, David, 17–18
Loveland Reporter-Herald, 63
Ludlow Massacre, 153–54, 161–64
Ludlow, Colorado, 153, 160–62,
    201–2

M

MacGregor, Alexander, 39, 46
Mallen, Perry M., 78
Martin, J. Gilman, 89
Masterson, William Barclay "Bat,"
    v, 69, 72, *73*, 74–75, 78, 79–80
Matchless Mine, 102
Maxey, Nathaniel, 95
May, Henry F., 173
Mazzulla, Fred, 145
McClure, Maj., 163
McKey, Tom, 76–77
McNight, Jim, 121
Means, Rice, 172–73, 188, 197
Mears, Otto, 63, 66
Meeker, Ralph, 49
Mesa Mountain, 8–9

Miller, Frank, 58, 60–61
Miller, James, 135–37
Miller, Victor, 139
Mills, Enos, 49
Mills, John Gillis, 81, 84–89
mining
    coal, 153–56, 165, 200–205
    in Estes Park, 40
    silver, 96–98, 102
Minniss, J. F., 89
Minor, George C., 172–73
Minute Men, 178, 189
Moffat, David, 98
Morgan, Alice, 98
Morley, Clarence, v, 172, 178, 186–
    87, 191, *192*, 193–98
Mormon Trail, 56

N

National Association for the
    Advancement of Colored People
    (NAACP), 183
Native Americans
    and Frémont expedition, 6,
        11, 13
    and Packer party, 57
    Sand Creek Massacre, 15,
        17–20, 22–23, 26–28
    See also specific tribes
New American Patriot, 189
New York Morning Telegraph, 79
Newlon, Col. Paul, 208
News (Denver), 111
Newton, Adj. Gen., 209
Nickell, Kels, 136–38
Nickell, Willie, 135–38, 140
Nicollet, Joseph, 4
Nimmo, John, 164
Noon, George, 56, 58
Norlin, George, 196
Normann, Martha Ann, 146
Nugent, James "Rocky Mountain
    Jim," v, 36, 43–51
Nutter, Preston, 56–57

223

About the Author

Phyllis J. Perry has lived in Boulder, Colorado, for forty years—within an hour's drive of Rocky Mountain National Park. She and her husband visit the park in all seasons of the year to photograph its beauties and to enjoy hiking, cross country skiing, fishing, and camping. Among her prize-winning books are *Animals Under the Ground* and *The Secrets of the Rock.* She is also the author of *A Kid's Look at Colorado*; *Sherlock Hounds: Our Heroic Search & Rescue Dogs*; *Sounds Around Us: Poems to Tickle Kids' Ears*; *The Alien, The Giant, and Rocketman*; and *Pandas' Earthquake Escape.* Perry is the author of *Colorado Fun* and *It Happened in Rocky Mountain National Park* (Globe Pequot).